RULES OF SPORTS AND GAMES

RULES OF SPORTS AND GAMES

Amitabh Suri

CRESCENT
PUBLISHING CORPORATION

Edition : 2021

ISBN: 978-81-8342-103-4

Published by:
CRESCENT PUBLISHING CORPORATION
4806/24, Mathur Lane,
Ansari Road, Darya Ganj,
New Delhi - 110 002
Ph.: 011 - 23244131
Mob.: + 91 - 9711991838, 9999021668
E-mail: crescentbook@gmail.com
Website: www.crescentpublishingcorp.weebly.com

Printed at:
Balaji Digital
Delhi

Preface

Sport and games are activities that are governed by a set of rules or customs and often engaged in competitively. These are used as entertainment for the player and the viewer. They have also been proven by experiments that daily exercise increases mental strength and power to study. These activities are also great for the body building muscle and losing weight.

Rules and laws for games and sports can vary from country to country and different sporting bodies can also play by variations of the official rules. This book contains the relevant information about the world famous sports. All the international sports and games are described with their brief historical background, skills and techniques and with the latest and amended rules and measurements with illustrations.

This book is specially intended for the teachers and students of physical education, prospective coaches, and for the general viewers having keen interest in the physical education and sports. It will definitely prove very useful for prospective coaches, professional sports persons, sportspersons of various sports and for those indulge in the field of sports and games.

Amitabh Suri

Contents

	Preface	*v*
1.	Meaning and Principles of Sports and Games	1
2.	Goals of Sports Education	15
3.	Games from Ancient to Modern Periods	79
4.	Asian Games	129
5.	Afro Asian Games	155
6.	Commonwealth Games	171
7.	Olympic Games	207
8.	International Charter of Physical Education and Sport	269
	Bibliography	279
	Index	281

1

Meaning and Principles of Sports and Games

Sport is a physical activity or skill carried out under a publicly agreed set of rules, and with a recreational purpose: for competition, for self-enjoyment, to attain excellence, for the development of skill, or some combination of these. The difference of purpose is what characterises sport, combined with the notion of individual (or team) skill or prowess.

A game is a recreational activity involving one or more players, defined by a goal that the players try to reach, and some set of rules that determines what the players can do. Games are played primarily for entertainment or enjoyment, but may also serve an educational or simulational role.

A game is a structured or semi-structured activity, usually undertaken for enjoyment and sometimes also used as an educational tool. (The term "game" is also used to describe simulation of various activities e.g., for the purposes of training, analysis or prediction, etc., see "Game (simulation)".) Games are generally distinct from work, which is usually carried out for remuneration, and from art, which is more concerned with the expression of ideas. However, the distinction is not clear-cut, and many games may also be considered work and/or art. An example of a game is chess. You use your brain(s) to solve the game and win the game. Key components of games are goals, rules, challenge, and interactivity. Games generally involve mental or physical stimulation, and often both. Many games help develop practical skills, serve as a form of exercise, or otherwise perform an educational, simulational or psychological role.

Known to have been played as far back as prehistoric times, games are a universal part of the human culture.

Tools

Games are often classified by the components required to play them (e.g. a ball, cards, a board and pieces or a computer). In places where the use of leather is well established, the ball has been a popular game piece throughout recorded history, resulting in a worldwide popularity of ball games such as rugby, basketball, football, cricket, tennis and volleyball. Other tools are more idiosyncratic to a certain region. Many countries in Europe, for instance, have unique standard decks of playing cards. Other games such as chess may be traced primarily through the development and evolution of its game pieces.

Many game tools are tokens, meant to represent other things. A token may be a pawn on a board, play money, or an intangible item such as a point scored. Games such as hide-and-seek or tag do not utilise any obvious tool. Rather its interactivity is defined by the environment. Games with the same or similar rules may have different gameplay if the environment is altered. For example, hide-and-seek in a school building differs from the same game in a park; an auto race can be radically different depending on the track or street course, even with the same cars.

Rules

Whereas games are often characterized by their tools, they are often defined by their rules. While rules are subject to variations and changes, enough change in the rules usually results in a "new" game. For instance, baseball can be played with "real" baseballs or with whiffleballs. However, if the players decide to play with only three bases, they are arguably playing a different game.

Rules generally determine turn order, the rights and responsibilities of the players, and each player's goals. Player rights may include when they may spend resources or move tokens. Common win conditions are being first to amass a certain quota of points or tokens (as in Settlers of Catan), having the greatest number of tokens at the end of the game (as in Monopoly), or some relationship of one's game tokens to those of one's opponent.

Ludwig Wittgenstein argued that language is a game consisting of tokens governed by rough-and-ready rules that arise by convention and are not strict.

Skill, Strategy, and Chance

A game's tools and rules will result in its requiring skill, strategy, chance or a combination thereof, and are classified accordingly. Games of skill include games of physical skill, such as wrestling, tug of war, hopscotch, target shooting, and stake and games of mental skill such as checkers and chess. Games of strategy include checkers, chess, go, arimaa, and tic-tac-toe, and often require special equipment to play them. Games of chance include gambling games (blackjack, mah jong, roulette etc.), as well as snakes and ladders and rock, paper, scissors; most require equipment such as cards or dice. However, most games contain two or all three of these elements. For example, American football and baseball involve both physical skill and strategy while poker and Monopoly combine strategy and chance.

Classification of Games

Games can be characterized by "what the player does." This is often referred to as gameplay, a term that arose among computer game designers in the 1980s but as of 2007 is starting to see use in reference to games of other forms. Major key elements identified in this context are tools and rules which define the overall context of game and which in turn produce skill, strategy, and chance.

Single-player Games

Most games require multiple players. However, Single-player games are unique in respect to the type of challenges a player faces. Unlike a game with multiple players competing with or against each other to reach the game's goal, a one-player game is a battle solely against an element of the environment (an artificial opponent), against one's own skills, against time or against chance. Playing with a yo-yo or playing tennis against a wall is not generally recognised as playing a game due to the lack of any formidable opposition. This is not true, though, for a single-player computer game where the computer provides opposition.

The following are the major groups of games, according to the nature and the mechanics of the element of gameplay, and the technological components aiding the process; there are the most competitive and nowadays professionally oriented field of sports, the traditional family-dedicated fun tabletop games with basic boards, tokens, cards or dice, and the other technologically advanced computer-processed video games.

Sports are arguably the most popular type of game. Many sports require special equipment and dedicated playing fields, leading to the involvement of a community much larger than the group of players. A city or town may set aside such resources for the organisation of sports leagues.

Popular sports may have spectators who are entertained just by watching games. A community will often align itself with a local sports team that supposedly represents it (even if the team or most of its players only recently moved in); they often align themselves against their opponents or have traditional rivalries. The concept of fandom began with sports fans.

Stanley Fish cited the balls and strikes of baseball as a clear example of social construction, the operation of rules on the game's tools. While the strike zone target is governed by the rules of the game, it epitomizes the category of things that exist only because people have agreed to treat them as real. No pitch is a ball or a strike until it has been labeled as such by an appropriate authority, the plate umpire, whose judgment on this matter cannot be challenged within the current game.

Certain competitive sports, such as racing and gymnastics, are not games by definitions such as Crawford's because competitors do not interact with their opponents.

Lawn Games

Lawn games are outdoor games that can be played on a lawn. Many games that are traditionally played on a pitch are marketed as "lawn games" for home use in a front or back yard. Common lawn games include Horseshoes, Croquet, Bocce and Stake.

Board games

Board games use as a central tool a board on which the players' status, resources, and progress are tracked using physical tokens. Many also involve dice and/or cards. Most games that simulate war are board games, and the board may be a map on which the players' tokens move. Some games, such as chess, are entirely deterministic, relying only on the strategy element for their interest. Children's games, on the other hand, tend to be very luck-based, with games such as Candy Land having virtually no decisions to be made. Trivia games have a great deal of randomness based on the questions a person gets. German-style board games are notable for often having rather less of a luck factor than many board games.

Card Games

Card games use as a central tool a deck of cards. The cards may be a standard Anglo-American (52-card) deck of playing cards (such as Go Fish or Crazy Eights, or a deck specific to the individual game (such as Set). Uno and Rook are examples of games that were originally played with a standard deck and have since been commercialized with customized decks.

Video Games

Video games are computer- or microprocessor-controlled games. Computers can create virtual tools to be used in a game, such as cards or dice, or far more elaborate worlds where mundane or fantastic things can be manipulated through gameplay.

A computer or video game uses one or more input devices, typically a button/joystick combination (on arcade games); a keyboard, mouse and/or trackball (computer games); or a controller or a motion sensitive tool. (console games). More esoteric devices such as paddle controllers have also been used for input. In computer games, the evolution of user interfaces from simple keyboard to mouse, joystick or joypad has profoundly changed the nature of game development.

In more open-ended computer simulations, aka sandbox-style games, notably those designed by Will Wright, the player may be free to do whatever they like within the confines of the virtual universe. Due to the lack of goals or opposition, it is disputed whether these programs are games or toys.

Online Games

Online games can be played in a browser anywhere, anytime the user has an Internet connection. Online games are popular across virtually all countries and age groups. Online games can be played with little or no experience. They generally invlove easy to use controls such as a mouse and keyboard. The simplicity and accesability of online games have made them extremely popular across the Internet.

Role-playing Games

Role-playing games, often abbreviated as RPGs, are a type of game in which the participants (usually) assume the roles of characters acting in a fictional setting. The original role playing games – or at least those explicitly marketed as such – are played with a handful of participants, usually face-to-face, and keeping track of the developing fiction with pen and paper. Together, the players may collaborate on a story involving those characters; create, develop, and "explore" the setting; or vicariously experience an adventure outside the bounds of everyday life. Pen-and-paper roleplaying games include, for example, Dungeons & Dragons and GURPS.

Modern independent RPGs, however, often blur the line between RPGs and board games or border on story-telling.

The term role playing game has also been appropriated by the video game industry to describe a genre of video games. These may be single-player games where one player experiences a programmed environment and story, or they may allow players to interact through the internet. The experience is usually quite different than traditional role playing games.

Sport is an activity that is governed by a set of rules or customs and often engaged in competitively. Used by itself, sports commonly refer to activities where the physical capabilities of the competitor are the sole or primary determiner of the outcome (winning or losing), but the term is also used to include activities such as mind sports and motor sports where mental acuity or equipment quality are major factors. Sports are used as entertainment for the player and the viewer. It has also been proven by experiments that daily exercise increases mental strength and power to study.

History

There are artefacts and structures that suggest that the Chinese engaged in sporting activities as early as 4000 BC. Gymnastics appears to have been a popular sport in China's ancient past. Monuments to the Pharaohs indicate that a number of sports, including swimming and fishing, were well-developed and regulated several thousands of years ago in ancient Egypt. Other Egyptian sports included javelin throwing, high jump, and wrestling. Ancient Persian sports such as the traditional Iranian martial art of Zourkhaneh had a close connection to the warfare skills. Among other sports that originate in Persia are polo and jousting.

A wide range of sports were already established by the time of Ancient Greece and the military culture and the development of sports in Greece influenced one another considerably. Sports became such a prominent part of their culture that the Greeks created the Olympic Games, which in ancient times were held every four years in a small village in the Peloponnesus called Olympia.

Sports have been increasingly organized and regulated from the time of the Ancient Olympics up to the present century. Industrialization has brought increased leisure time to the citizens of developed and developing countries, leading to more time for citizens to attend and follow spectator sports, greater participation in athletic activities, and increased accessibility. These trends continued with the advent of mass media and global communication. Professionalism became prevalent, further adding to the increase in sport's popularity, as sports fans began following the exploits of professional athletes through radio, television, and the internet—all while enjoying the exercise and competition associated with amateur participation in sports.

In the new millennium, new sports have been going further from the physical aspect to the mental or psychological aspect of competing. Cyber sports organizations are becoming more and more popular. Activities where the outcome is determined by judgement over execution are considered performances, or competition.

Sportsmanship

Sportsmanship is an attitude that strives for fair play, courtesy toward teammates and opponents, ethical behaviour and integrity, and grace in losing. Sportsmanship expresses an aspiration or ethos that the activity will be enjoyed for its own sake. The well-known sentiment by sports journalist Grantland Rice, that it's "not that you won or lost but how you played the game," and the Modern Olympic creed expressed by its founder Pierre de Coubertin: "The most important thing . . . is not winning but taking part" are typical expressions of this sentiment.

But often the pressures of competition or an obsession with individual achievement—as well as the intrusion of technology—can all work against enjoyment and fair play by participants. People responsible for leisure activities often seek recognition and respectability as sports by joining sports federations such as 5 IOC, or by forming their own regulatory body. In this way sports evolve from leisure activity to more formal sports: relatively recent newcomers are BMX cycling, snowboarding, and wrestling. Some of these activities have been popular but uncodified pursuits in various forms for different lengths of time. Indeed, the formal regulation of sport is a relatively modern and increasing development.

Sportsmanship, within any given game, is how each competitor acts before, during, and after the competition. Not only is it important to have good sportsmanship if one wins, but also if one loses. For example, in football it is considered sportsmanlike to kick the ball out of play to allow treatment for an injured player on the other side. Reciprocally, the other team is expected to return the ball from the throw-in.

Violence in sports involves crossing the line between fair competition and intentional aggressive violence. Athletes, coaches, fans, and parents sometimes unleash violent behaviour on people or property, in misguided shows of loyalty, dominance, anger, or celebration. Rioting or hooliganism are common and ongoing problems at national and international sporting contests, particularly football matches.

Professionalism

The entertainment aspect of sports, together with the spread of mass media and increased leisure time, has led to professionalism in sports. This has resulted in some conflict, where the paycheck can be seen as more important than recreational aspects, or where the sports are changed simply to make them more profitable and popular, thereby losing certain valued traditions.

The entertainment aspect also means that sportsmen and women are often elevated to celebrity status.

Politics

At times, sports and politics can have a large amount of influence on each other.

When apartheid was the official policy in South Africa, many sports people adopted the conscientious approach that they should not appear in competitive sports there. Some feel this was an effective contribution to the eventual demolition of the policy of apartheid, others feel that it may have prolonged and reinforced its worst effects. The 1936 Summer Olympics held in Berlin was an illustration, perhaps best recognised in retrospect, where an ideology was developing which used the event to strengthen its spread through propaganda.

In the history of Ireland, Gaelic sports were connected with cultural nationalism. Until the mid 20th century a person could have been banned from playing Gaelic football, hurling, or other sports administered by the Gaelic Athletic Association (GAA) if she/he played or supported soccer, or other games seen to be of British origin. Until recently the GAA continued to ban the playing of soccer and rugby union at Gaelic venues. This ban is still enforced, but has been modified to allow football and rugby be played in Croke Park while Lansdowne Road is being redeveloped. Until recently, under Rulé 21, the GAA also banned members of the British security forces and members of the RUC from playing Gaelic games, but the advent of the Good Friday Agreement in 1998 led to the eventual removal of the ban.

Nationalism is often evident in the pursuit of sports, or in its reporting: people compete in national teams, or commentators and audiences can adopt a partisan view. On occasion, such tensions can lead to violent confrontation among players or spectators within and beyond the sporting venue (see Football War). These trends are seen by many as contrary to the fundamental ethos of sports being carried on for its own sake and for the enjoyment of its participants.

Physical Art

Sports have many affinities with physical art. Ice skating and Tai chi, and nowadays Dancesport for example, are sports that come close to artistic spectacles in themselves. Similarly, there are other activities that have elements of sport and art in their execution, such as artistic gymnastics, Bodybuilding, Parkour, performance art, Yoga, bossaball, dressage, culinary arts, etc. Perhaps the best example is Bull-fighting, which in Spain is reported in the arts pages of newspapers. The fact that art is so close to sports in some situations is probably related to the nature of sports. The definition of "sports" above put forward the idea of an activity pursued not just for the usual purposes, for example, running not simply to get places, but running for its own sake, running as well as we can.

This is similar to a common view of aesthetic value, which is seen as something over and above the strictly functional value coming from an object's normal use. So an aesthetically pleasing car is one which doesn't just get from A to B, but which impresses us with its grace, poise, and charisma.

In the same way, a sporting performance such as jumping doesn't just impress us as being an effective way to avoid obstacles or to get across streams. It impresses us because of the ability, skill, and style which is shown.

Art and sports were probably more clearly linked at the time of Ancient Greece, when gymnastics and callisthenics invoked admiration and aesthetic appreciation for the physical build, prowess and 'arete' displayed by participants. The modern term 'art' as skill, is related to this ancient Greek term 'arete'. The closeness of art and sport in these times was revealed by the nature of the Olympic Games which, as we have seen, were celebrations of both sporting and artistic achievements, poetry, sculpture and architecture.

Technology

Golf, a kind fo sports where the moving has much lesser part than dexterity has.

Technology has an important role in sports, whether applied to an athlete's health, the athlete's technique, or equipment's characteristics.

Equipment As sports have grown more competitive, the need for better equipment has arose. Golf clubs, football helmets, baseball bats, soccer balls, hockey skates, and other equipment have all seen considerable changes when new technologies have been applied.

Health Ranging from nutrition to the treatment of injuries, as the knowledge of the human body has deepened over time, an athlete's potential has been increased. Athletes are now able to play to an older age, recover more quickly from injuries, and train more effectively than previous generations of athletes.

Instruction Advancing technology created new opportunities for research into sports. It is now possible to analyse aspects of sports that were previously out of the reach of comprehension. Being able to use motion capture to capture an athlete's movement, or advanced computer simulations to model physical scenarios has greatly increased an athlete's ability to understand what they are doing and how they can improve themselves.

2

Goals of Sports Education

A comprehensive, articulated physical education system helps children and youths achieve three goals. Within each goal appropriate disciplines are addressed to support the knowledge, skills, and attitudes desired for every student. The three goals are equally important; each interacts continually with the others in a well-planned program. The following skill and content areas support the goals of physical education and are introduced at appropriate ages and grade levels. In addition to developing skills in these various areas, students should be encouraged to acquire understanding and knowledge about the content and skills.

Following are the basis of content areas are physical education:

- Rhythms and Dance
- Individual and Dual Sports
- Aquatics
- Team Sports Combatives
- Effects of Physical Activity on Dynamic Health
- Outdoor Education
- Gymnastics and Tumbling

These skill and content areas are the basis of physical education. For example, developing a sense of rhythm helps children do better in a variety of activities and enhances a sense of flow and coordination. At all levels of the physical education curriculum, the skill areas are taught and reinforced through the content. Cognitive learning is an inherent part of the skill and content areas.

Students learn the application of Newton's laws in developing rotational skills, balance, and spin. This knowledge helps to reinforce and strengthen their understanding of the skills and their ability to use them. Throughout the physical education curriculum, children should be encouraged to observe their own and others ' behaviour and to process information. Although children do learn through trial and error, they also benefit from guided discovery and development of an understanding of skills and content.

Myths About Physical Education

Physical education is a multifaceted process that teaches a wide range of skills and activities with the aim of the students ' becoming physically educated, physically fit, able to enjoy a variety of physical activities, and committed to lifelong health and physical well-being. It is a continuing process of articulated, sequential development of skills, talents, attitudes, and behaviours. Physical education is not an integral part of the school's curriculum. Physical education is closely connected to and supports the other disciplines. Physical education is an integral component of the school curriculum. It involve students directly in thinking, creating meaning, and learning how to learn.

Physical education focuses on the more athletically gifted. All children have the potential to become physically educated, and an effective physical education program will reach all children regardless of their talents, skills, or limitations. Physical education should be similar to training -highly skill-and drill-oriented. It should be mainly a mechanical process.

In physical education emphasis must be placed on a broad spectrum of learning and personal development. Learning involves thinking and feeling, being active and processing information, not just using skills. Education encompasses much more than training. Children should carry out a variety of physical fitness activities but do not need to understand why they are doing so.

Learning cognitively is as important to physical education as learning specific movement skills. Students need to know why they are learning skills in physical education and how they are benefiting personally. Then they will be more likely to accept responsibility for improving skills on their own and enjoying the benefits of physical education over the long term. Physical education programs may be detrimental to doing one's best in a particular activity. It is important to focus on a specific activity (or sport) in order to do really well.

A well-planned, comprehensive physical education system helps children and youths develop all their abilities and talents rather than focus exclusively on a narrow range. Because children change and grow over time, they should be encouraged to become well rounded. They should be encouraged to become proficient in and appreciate a wide variety of physical activities from which they can choose wisely. Because there are always winners and losers in games and sports, physical education must emphasize competition to prepare children for participation in the real world.

Although teachers are aware of the nature of competition, they do not require higher levels of competition from children before they are ready. Further, competition can take different forms. Activities in physical education programs may emphasize self-improvement, participation, and cooperation instead of winning or losing.

A well-planned physical education program is sequential, developmental, and age-appropriate. An effective physical education program should be governed by the vision for physical education described. It does not consist of just games and sports. An effective physical education program balances and contributes to children's academic learning. It is not separate and distinct from the core curriculum. Neither is participation in a specialized athletic sport an adequate substitute for a comprehensive physical education system.

Physical education programs should help children and youths develop a lifelong commitment to their own physical well-being, health, and fitness, with a clear emphasis on a variety of pleasurable physical activities and an active life-style.

There are three goals for central to an effective physical education program. No single goal should be emphasized to the exclusion of the other goals. Schools need to have a well-planned and well-supported physical education program for children in kindergarten through grade twelve. To do so requires a commitment of leadership, staff, and resources.

In contemporary usage physical implies the medium through which the education takes place. One acquires an education in many ways and from many sources, not only through reading books but also the through other important experiences. The adjective physical does not imply that we are educating the physical, *i.e.,* developing physical powers or cultivating physical skills solely for their own sakes. Modern physical education sees these skills more as a means to an end than as absolute or continuing ends in themselves.

As a matter of fact there are very few movements performed, or skills developed, which are persisted in merely for their own value, even in infancy and childhood.As soon as a goal is desired the movement or skill needed to attain it is practiced.

The child who wants the cookie learns to walk over and get it. A child learns to ride a bicycle not just in order to ride the bicycle but to preserve status with the gang, go to school, or show off.

Physical training is an older but still used term to describe the training of the physical components of the body without any necessary reference to the purposes which are significant in modern education. It should not be confused with physical education.

They are not synonymous, as we shall see in the chapter which follow. Nor should the term physical education be allowed to imply a separation from the mental and thus perpetuate the unfortunate but traditional notion that man exists as mind and body, and that education is concerned with only one, or at the most two, of these parts. The concept of man as a unified being makes confusion on this score unnecessary.

Physical education serves as a medium for man's total education, intellectual, emotional, developmental, using experiences centered in movement. And in today's schools these experiences are focused largely on the natural movements of active play or recreational life.

Physical Experience

It is difficult indeed to describe what a physical experience is, or what physical education. Man does not exist as a physical self-differentiated from his mental or spiritual self. He is thus unable to have physical experience unrelated to other phases of his life. Some may feel that a swim in a cool lake is something physical, but actually the whole organism is involved—in terms of feelings, choice of stroke or distance, reflections on previous dangers, or necessary precautions. The boy who hits his first home run is surely undergoing more than merely physical change brought about by swimming the bat or running the bases.

Every human experience is a magnificent mixture. We may identify one element as more prominent than another, but we misunderstand the nature of experience whenever we regard any act as exclusively composed of the quality with which we attempt to endow it. Experience is an interaction of the whole organism with its environment, and the environment includes other persons as well as traditions, customs, and the local physical surroundings.

Indeed, so clear is this fact that medicine, jurisprudence, and education have re-written their practices in order to take into account the total situation—the individual reacting to and interacting with all the forces of the environment that play upon the materials of man. Because every experience embodies the reaction and interaction of the individual to and with his environment, the experience cannot be purely physical or purely mental.

Only the need for identification breaks experience into categories such as spiritual, mental, social, moral, intellectual, or physical. These are terms of conventence and largely without reality. Although common sense recognizes that one factor may be dominant, it is never wholly exclusive... We shall keep the balance even if we remember that the physical experience is physical in its outward manifestation but mental and emotional, social and moral, in its relationships and meanings... One may not like the physical but it remains, permanent and abiding, going on from generation to generation.

If education aims to improve the quality of living, one must be careful in judging just where quality is to be found. It is not merely the fine arts which may lay claims to qualitative experience. Indeed, John Dewey believed that the qualitative, the fine, the potentially uplifting perwaded every experience—a ball game, a symphony, a business transaction, or whatever. So, in suggesting that the physical experience has qualitative aspects, can we be more specific about its nature and its place in the development of mankind? We believe so. We believe four of its contributions can be identified.

Experience in Expression

Mountain climbers are frequently, asked why they persist in climbing mountains. Perhaps the best answer was given by Maliory, who climbed Everest, when he said, "We climbed it because it was there." He expressed his inner urges by mastering that particularly hazardous mountain. It was something to be done and he did it. Never mind the utilitarian value.

Perhaps there was none. Perhaps he proved nothing—to anyone else. But to himself he expressed much. It is the same thing when the painter paints. He has to. His whole purpose in life will be unitifilied if he doesn't. And so it is with the child who plays. He has to. In play he expresses not only those things which are within him but the cultural patterns he has been brought up in as well. A child at play will reveal not only some of his cultural background but his personality—his worries, fears, and fantasies; his ambitions, hopes, and concerns; and his joy, exaltation, or disappointment.

Experience in Appreciation

Many a competitive yachtsman has had difficulty keeping his mind on his mainsail and tiller because of the temptation to enjoy to the fullest the beauty of the water, the colour, or the configuration of sails as they pass under scudding clouds.To enjoy and appreciate "the wonders which nature hath wrought" is one of the great rewards of the effort is takes to seek a particular vantage point in the Grand Canyon or to walk the beach at night to see the phosphorescent glow of the plankton left on the sand by the receding wave. To watch the grace and rhythm, dexterity and speed, courage and verve of a magnificent athlete or artist in dance is an experience in appreciation.

The pleasure the spectator derives from sports can be immeasurably enriched when he is taught to enjoy something other than merely the score of the game. One's awareness of the beauty of performance, the intelligence of strategy, the daring and skill of the competitors is enhanced if he himself participates in a sport. To experience the thrill of the ski run, the "zing" of the runners on the snow, the rush of the wind, the breathlessness of the sharp drop is one of life's real joys. Not always in modern physical education are the brittle and transitory values displayed on the scoreboard the only ones talked of or held highly.

An appreciation of skill no matter where it is found, a cultivated friendship from the field of play, some understanding of the opponent and his way of life—these are additional benefits which derive from "physical" experience. President Bixler of Colby College mentions as one of the rewards of a good liberal education a student's development of "habits of discriminating thinking which will enable him to sift..the good and the beautiful from the cheap and the shoddy." This sort of appreciation has great meaning for modern physical education. The teacher can seek the good and the beautiful in performance and in behaviour and renounce, by teaching and example, all that is cheap and shoddy.

Experience in Learning

It is clear that over the centuries educators have reckoned with physical education but have never been quite sure of its value or place. They have, in the main, conceived of learning as possible only through eyes and ears in the quite contemplation of a page or through listening to a teacher. Formal teaching started with physical education. It was only after physical training had reached a fairly highly developed form in the Greek gymnasium that other subjects were included, and these institutions are the forerunners of the modern academies and colleges. How much a child learned the first time he climbed a tree-about the distant field he saw, the nest he gazed into, about him as he attained the dizzy height, or about his playmate who was afraid to climb—would be difficult to understand, to organize, and to reduce to the usual academic formulas of the classroom and lecture hall.

To appreciate fully the deep exaltation which comes form triumph in a child's relay race or a big-time football game, or, conversely, to experience, analyze, and profit from the disappointment attendant upon the loss of such matches, is to understand something of the real opportunity of teaching of the real opportunity for teaching about life and the way it can be lived. The capacity for movement, for climbing trees and throwing balls, is a capacity for learning. We learn because we can move from place to place. Movement is a means of gaining experience. It is an avenue of learning so universal and so important as to defy neglect. How far bac!· in life does such learning go? In the evolutionary scheme of things it goes back to the one-celled amoeba.

As this flowing mite of protoplasm sends out its "feelers," its, pseudopodia, it may strike danger or food. The amoeba cannot be said to have "learned" the difference, in the sense that it will make a choice next time, but because it could move it thus developed and lived and mastered its highly restricted environment. The baby robin or the kitten or the colt learns a great deal of its world by moving about. It learns where refuge is, and food. It learns as much as it can, not from books, but by fusing all its resources of sight, smell, hearing, movement into one. So it is with man.

His physical education is not solely what Plato called it—exercise or sports aimed at the cultivation of the soul. We have spoken of one's physical education as the sum of those experience which come to him through movement. If a child crawls across the floor and bumps his head on the table leg, he learns that table legs are hard and to be avoided. Such is part of his physical education. If, when he is four, he falls from the garage roof, he has learned something about height and danger and the hardness of the earth.

His physical education is progressing. Later, when he becomes a man and loses a golf match, he may have learned the futility of the alibi and thus be regarded by his fellows as a "good sport" and by a psychiatrist as a well-balanced and well integrated individual.

We only become confused about physical education when we debate its purposes, political or otherwise, or when we argue over whether to grant academic credit for it in a modern school. These are merely questions for academicians.

The physical education of a child goes on whether in school or out, with or without credit, sanctioned or unsanctioned. It is fundamental to life, or growth, and to development. The truly important question is, how are we to control or to organize this contribution, which inevitably will be made to human development in order to bring about planned or desired results in human behaviour?

Early Movement Patterns

Movement patterns begin in infancy. Certainly movement is essential before birth; usually its absence is cause for alarm. The random kicking and thrusting of the newborn infant is his way of attempting to adapt to the alien environment in which he finds himself; and rather rapidly, the kicks and thrusts take on meaning in terms of the baby's disposition and personality. In a dozen weeks or so after birth, the infant attempts an almost systematic investigation of his surroundings and quickly establishes himself in a position where his movement commands attention. Thus do infants grow, interpreting their life needs through their gross movement patterns and demanding a pivotal place in the family circle. The toddler uses total bodily movement as his means of expression and communication. Before abstract ideas can be transmitted through language, the baby has usually conditioned his household to an extensive vocabulary through a multitude of movement patterns which more than adequately convey his desires.

The banging spoon on the high-chair tray, the incessant jerking of the crib railing, the upraised arms, the head hidden in the pillow—all carry connotations which the majority of parents recognize instantly. The preschool youngster moves to a great extent as he is directed to move, but he continues to retain an individuality of expression and his movements not only teach him who he is but seem to carry with them the joy of living as well. Running just to run, jumping just to jump, throwing just to throw—these are part of the young child's life, and the joy of this nondirected movement is spontaneous and effervescent. As the young human matures toward adolescence, his movement patterns become more restrained and also more refined.

The elementary school youngster wants his movements to have certain patterns that are usable in terms of games, acquatics, and self-testing activities. He jumps to see how far he can jump, he throws to see how accurately he can throw, he runs to see how fast he can run. Each movement pattern is a mode of self-discovery. The child learns about others as well as himself and he often measures his understandings in terms of gross bodily movement. To know that Sammy can run faster than he can tells the child a great deal about a life situation that will be encountered in hundreds of different ways.

The almost animal nature of elementary school children explodes in movement that cannot be denied, even if society should see fit to try to restrict it. The adolescent has been sufficiently socialized to recognize that unrestricted movement is no longer acceptable as a pattern of behaviour. He must find ways to move in accordance with the tenets of his culture. Often organized games, aquatics, and dance are the most suitable outlets, and it is during adolescence that games achieve a real significance as part of the socialization process.

Athletic contests and all of their concomitant actions will supply the movement which the organism seems to demand. Providing there has been the opportunity available to acquire basic skill, the average adolescent seeks socially acceptable ways to give vent to his desires to move. Some children learn to express themselves very adequately through gross movement, some continue to use movement as a way of effecting self-discovery, many use it as a method of interrelating with others, and some adolescents establish status in group situations through movement.

At this particular stage, it is possible to condition the adolescent to believe either that movement is to be associated with the concept of childishness or that it is to be regarded in the light of maturity. By adulthood, man has been molded so carefully by his society that he comes to accept certain standards withouc question. American social standards tend to emphasize the concept that restricted movement, and indeed idleness, indicates: social maturity which is desirable. Not all culture agree.

The British culture emphasizes the merit of movement in the form of games, the German stresses the importance of movement for national fitness, the Scandinavian focuses attention on movement as an adjunct to health. But in the United States, th re is a tendency to relegate patterns of acti /ity to the "professional" or to the immature. Obviously there are a number of exceptions to such a generalization.

Organic Factors

All of education is interested in taking the individual where he is and helping him realize what he may become. In no other phase of life can this goal be actualized more dramatically than in human organic development. Physical education programmes are based on the physical educator's understanding of the human being and his capacities and limitations. It is imperative for the competent physical educator to have a thorough understanding of the tool with which he is working. It might be argued reasonably that it is not necessary for a good physical education teacher to be a physiologist, but he must have a strong foundation in the biological and behavioral sciences in order best to work with man himself.

In the same way, it might be argued that one need not be a mechanic in order to drive a car; but driving is only one aspect of automotive knowledge, just as the rules, skills, and strategy of games, aquatics, and dance are only part of physical education knowledge. Once something starts to happen to the car, it is essential to find a mechanic, and once something starts to happen to man through activity, it is essential that there be on hand a physical educator well grounded to the "why" as well as the "what" and "how". The most accurate generalization that can be made about man is that individual differences far outweigh individual similarities. No two persons, not even identical twins, are exactly alike.

One of the most important factors influencing man's structure is his hereditary background. Each individual is endowed with certain gene combinations inherited from his parents, and the combinations are so limitless that children in the same family often have different physiques, different colouring and different structural identities. However, within the limits of his hereditary background, the individual has a tremendous opportunity to develop or inhibit his potentialities. Variation in heredity means variations of physique: gross differences in height and weight, in muscle and fat, and in degrees of flexibility.

The teacher of physical education must be aware of such genetic factors within individuals and adjust his programme accordingly.

Growth and Development

Although it is known that man follows a patterned growth cycle, one cannot always predict accurately at what stage a person should be at a specific chronological age. According to Shuttleworth, the child has a period of rapid growth from birth to about age 6. Then a plateau is hit, when he continues to grow, but not as fast as during the first five or six years. This is followed by the pubescent growth spurt, which usually occurs anywhere between 10 and 15 years of age. Then the growth cycle tapers off with another plateau, until maturity of physique is attained.

Many girls have a tendency to mature more rapidly than the majority of boys, so that pubescence or the onset of menstruation usually occurs in females in the North American climate at about the age of 11-13, while the secondary sex characteristics of boys in the North American climate generally appear at about the age of 14-16. Within each sex there are early maturers and late matures, and this condition is not completely predictable. Hence, it is possible to find in a single age group a variety of growth differences, some due to heredity and others to individual growth patterns.

This variation is especially pronounced in the sixth and seventh grades. Here a late-maturing little girl, who has no secondary sex characteristics, who has not reached her growth spurt, and who gives the appearance of a child, may be seated right beside a young girl who has already started her menstrual periods, who has many secondary sex characteristics, who has already achieved her maximum height, and who looks like a very young woman. In the same class might be the early-maturing boy whose voice has changed, who seems as arms and legs, who is quite tall and muscular, and who is beginning to grow a soft fuzz on his face. By his side is a chubby and cherubic little boy with a high shrill voice, who has not yet started his pubescent growth spurt but whose appearance believes his age.

Among these examples the variation may be as much as 12 inches in height and 50 pounds in weight; yet all of the children are in the same class and are of the same chronological age. Obviously, there will be many,

many children in this age group who are between the extremes suggested and who will be called "average" in height, weight, and growth. The teacher of physical education must be constantly aware that these extremes are not "abnormal." Although the deviation presents a problem, that problem can be solved with knowledge and understanding.

The deviant child tends to feel different from his group and if physical education activities attempt to capitalize on that difference, or ignore it, some personality problem may develop. Too often, class standing and age are the basis for classification in physical education classes: thus, all seventh graders participate in the same physical education programme regardless of their physique and growth pattern. A more realistic classification has been attempted through assignment of activities on the basis of height and weight. While this is a relatively easy criterion to apply and does eliminate some of the inequalities of age classification, it would be even wiser and sounder to attempt to classify on skill ability as well as physique. Many mature small boys are put with not-yet-mature big boys on the theory that all are the same size and hence equal. However, the matured youngster is usually the more skilled youngster and the "little" boy is often penalized because his skill ability has not been taken into account. Too often physical education teachers ignore the late growers and concentrate on the early growers.

Consequently, certain children are over-looked and do not receive skill training when they should. For example, the late-growing boy is ignored in favour of the early grower in seventh-grade basketball. When the late maturer attains his growth spurt, say in the tenth grade, he could very well exceed the early grower in height, weight, and muscle and thus have the potential to be excellent basketball player.

However, if his acquisition of skills was not fostered, his ability is limited and usually he is not interested in "catching up" with his more skilled, but shorter and lighter, early-growing friend. Girls, too, seem to be penalized if they display a growth differential. If they are early growers, their inability to fit into the group because of their size seems to foster an insecurity which is difficult to eradicate. This may be accentuated because so few of the sports and games for girls are based upon strength, as are the boys' games, and while maturity usually brings strength, it is not necessarily accompanied by either ability or flexibility.

Girls who are teased excessively about their early maturity tend to become somewhat introverted and often attempt to avoid physical activity so that their bodies need not be displayed. It must be remembered that although a girl looks like a mature young woman she is still a child in her attitudes, understanding, and interests. The physical educator will expect neither exceptional performance nor exemplary behaviour from the early-maturing girl. Instead, he will try to help her, through activity, to accept herself and her growth pattern. Another problem which is especially bothersome is the fact that girls in the pubescent age group tend to be taller and heavier than their brothers. Very often this means that the girl is also stronger and has greater endurance.

This physical advantage plays havoc with some social customs and may even cause psychological problems. Contests which involve both strength and endurance, such as team games, may accord the girls an advantage. In view of the social structure which expects greater strength and endurance from the male, most team sports of a coeducational nature are not desirable during pubescence; instead, flexibility and balance should be emphasized in some activities, such as social dancing, it may be wise to group girls with boys older than themselves so that size differential does not become an embarrassing factor. Activities in aquatics, self-testing, dance, and rhythms are all excellent for coeducational programmes. The physical educator will understand reticence during this particular period and will not attempt to accentuate sexual differences.

Body Build

There has long been an interest among some physical educators in classifying humans according to various types of body build. The classification proposed by William Sheldon, based on the process of somatotyping, has been generally accepted. This process separate people into three groups:

Endomorph—heavy set, square, fat, rounded type.

Mesomorph—athletic, muscular, well-developed type.

Ectomorph—thin, long, angular type.

Naturally there are intermediate groups and Sheldon's classification process is much more complicated than the above categories would indicate. Sheldon judges the individual on a point scale of 1 through 7 and then proceeds to assess body segments, giving a detailed and lucid picture of body build. Interestingly, somatotyping has only limited use, and then usually with men.

The mammary development of girls does not necessarily follow physique indications, yet it has marked effect upon structure and function. In addition, men and women tend to gather adipose tissue indifferent patterns, so that the female has a different structure from that of the male. Women accumulate far easily on hips and thighs, whereas men usually gain fatty tissue around the waist and lower thorax. The female fat deposits tend to distort the somatotype classification; that is the appearance of endomorphy might be given while in reality the individual being classified is a slightly obese mesomorph.

All else being equal, it is usually the mesomorph who excels in athletics although a number of sports cater to the other two body types. Wrestling, for example, in certain aspects seems to favour the endomorphic build, and track gives an advantage to the ectomorphic type. Boxing is a typical example of a sport which attempts to take body build into consideration.

Basketball is geared to the tall player and inflicts a penalty on the short one. The physical education teacher should be ready to help solve problems relative to physique and growth patterns. Sometimes this means forming teams according to height, sometimes building teams on skill classifications, sometimes basing team selection on weight. It would be wise to analyze the components of the game and attempt to select teams on a basis that did not give unfair advantage to anyone because of structural traits. It might behoove physical education to look more closely as its programme and to plan it so that allowances for different body builds are made in many activities. Not the least of the tasks of the wise physical educator is to help the student understand and accept his hereditary physique and to feel comfortable with it.

Many a young man has lived a tortured life because he was "too short"; many a young woman has felt socially inept because she was "too tall". Shortness, tallness smallness, heaviness; fat legs, slim hips, broad shoulders, pleasing curves are modifiable only to a certain extent. There is a point at which a person must learn to accept himself as he is, and not long instead for what he wishes he were. An intelligent physical educator can emphasize the concept of "feeling comfortable in your own skin" and thus contribute to a general self-acceptance which in many cases is the basis of sound physical and emotional well-being. There are many who look to physical education to produce balanced, beautiful bodies—the bodies of Greek gods—a symmetrical perfection of human form.

Physical education can make some contribution toward a well-functioning being but it does not guarantee symmetry or claim to produce Greek gods. The body is not symmetrical and beauty is relative at best. The cults of the Atlas producers, the body-beautiful gymnasiums, the beauty salons utilize certain physical exercises to attain the end which they advertise, but exercise is only one of their "props." Steam baths, massage, beauty consultation, and diet assist in achieving the advertised ideal.

Physical education, on the other hand, is interested in presenting a programme of directed movement which will enhance the total well-being of the participant and facilitate the development of beauty of function. The "props" used by physical educators are understanding of the biological and behavioural nature of man and a philosophy which envisions him as a totality.

Environment Needed for a Quality Physical Education Programme

Supportive environment is important to the success of the overall physical education program. Support for physical education should include the following elements:

- Physical education is recognized as an integral part of the school curriculum.
- Physical education continually supports and interacts with other subject areas.
- Physical education is included as part of a planned staff development program.
- Facilities, equipment, and supplies are provided that are safe and adequate.

- The psychological environment enables and encourages all students to succeed in physical education.
- The physical education program involves the school, the home, and the community.

As an integral part of the school curriculum, physical education should be taught by qualified professionals who have been trained in physical education or who have participated in a program of professional development focusing on the teaching of physical education.

Classes for children and youths with special needs or disabilities should be taught by physical education teachers who know how to design and implement programs for such students. A quality physical education program provides equal access for all students and guarantees opportunities for maximum participation, optimum development, and appropriate individual attention. Opportunities for personal attention, individualized instruction, and time on task should be included.

Physical education teachers should be encouraged to participate on school or district interdisciplinary teams to develop the physical education curriculum. In a well-planned program the physical education teacher assumes responsibility for (1) implementing the physical education curriculum; (2) relating physical education to other subject areas; (3) working with other professionals to create interdisciplinary approaches to learning; and (4) promoting the cooperation of school, home, and community in providing the highest-quality physical education experience possible for every student.

Physical education should continually support and interact with the other subject areas. For example, in its emphasis on personal health and the need for a healthy life-style, physical education reinforces but does not supplant health education. Teachers of physical education and health education should work together to integrate their curricula to reinforce the importance of maintaining an active and healthy life-style. Both can emphasize skills related to refusing negative pressures and influences, resolving conflicts,and coping with pressure, all of which are necessary for positive social interaction and healthy development.

Physical education classes provide a natural environment for the development of personal and social skills transferable to other situations and learning in other subject areas. There is a natural correlation, for example, between cooperative learning activities related to understanding the place of rules and strategies in physical education and the teaching of civic values, rights, and responsibilities in history -social science.

Continual interaction should occur between teachers of physical education and the rest of the staff. Through this interaction physical education and the other disciplines support and reinforce one other. Other examples of integration with the rest of the curriculum include the following:

- *Natural sciences* -through concepts related to gravity, levers, motion, physics, anatomy, biomechanics, and exercise physiology
- *Home economics* -through the study of exercise physiology and nutrition
- *History* -social science -through an emphasis on guiding students to become active, productive members of a democratic society; work cooperatively in groups and teams; and develop an understanding of others through cross-cultural and multicultural games, dances, and other activities

- *English* -language arts -through applying physical education experiences in written assignments and other activities requiring communication skills
- *Mathematics* -through recording results and calculating probabilities, percentages, and averages related to physical activity or creating graphs to demonstrate measurements and comparisons of personal progress
- *Visual and performing arts* -through a shared emphasis on aesthetic perception, creative expression, rhythm, tempo, and meter
- *Career* -vocational education -through the study of careers in such areas as teaching, recreation, health, fitness, dance performance, and sports broadcasting As emphasized throughout this framework ,physical education includes more than the education of the physical body. All subject areas should function as integrated components in the education of the total individual.

Physical education classes provide a natural environment for the development of personal and social skills transferable to other situations and learning in other subject areas.

School Health Programme

The ultimate objectives of school health and physical education programmes are similar. The essential difference lies in the fact that each area attempts to achieve its goals by utilizing different skills, media, and approaches.

The long-term, over-all objective of a health programme is to maintain and improve the health of human beings. This refers to all aspects of health, including physical, mental, emotional, and social. It applies to all individuals, regardless of race, colour, economic status, creed, or national origin.

The school has responsibility to see that all students achieve and maintain optimum health, not only from a legal point of view but also from the standpoint that the educational experience will be much more meaningful if optimum health exists. A child learns easier and better when in a state of good health. Some specific objectives established for the School Health Programme as stated by the Illinois Joint Committee on School Health are as follows:

- To inspire the child with a desire to be well and happy; To convey to the child a public and personal health ideal, designed to ensure for liar the continuation throughout life of wholesome and effective living, physical and mental;
- To educate the child, according to a definite plan, in the cultivation of those habits of living which will promote his present and his future health:
- To impart health knowledge and attitudes to the child so that he will make intelligent health decisions;
- To develop in the child a scientific attitude toward health matters, and an understanding of the scientific approach to health problems;
- To maintain adequate sanitation in the school, the home, and the community;
- To protect the child against communicable and preventable diseases and physical defects by providing effective public health control measures, both individual and social, throughout the school and the community;
- To bring each child up to his own optimal level of health;

- To extend the school health programme into the home by obtaining family and community support for the programme;
- To discover early and physical defects the child may have, secure their correction to the extent that they are remediable, and assist the child to adapt himself to any residual handicap;
- To provide healthful school living for the child;
- To relate the school health programme to the health programme in the community so that it may deal with real, current, and practical problems;
- To organize effectively not only the programme of direct health instruction but the equally important indirect learning experiences of the child in the field of health.

Turner lists the major objectives of the school health programme as the achievement of optimal pupil health through:

- The correction of physical defects.
- The reduction of communicable disease.
- The development of healthful school living.
- The interpretation of the school health programme to home and the development of home and school cooperation.
- The development and maintenance of desirable health habits.
- The development of health knowledge.
- The development of desirable mental attitudes toward health, health practices, and life situations.

Objectives of the School Physical Education Programme

A study of the individual reveals four general directions or phases in which growth and development take place, namely, physical development, motor development, mental development, and human relations development.

Physical education plays an important part in contributing to each of these phases of human growth and development. The physical development objective deals with the programme of activities which builds physical power in an individual through the development of the various organic systems of the body.

It results in the ability to sustain adaptive effort, the ability to recover, and the ability to resist fatigue. The value of this objective is based on the fact that an individual will be more active, have better performance, and be healthier, if the systems of the body are adequately developed and functioning properly.

Muscular activity plays a major role in the development of the organic systems of the body. The term "organic" refers to the digestive, circulatory, excretory, heat regulatory, respiratory, and other systems of the human body.

These systems are stimulated and trained through such activities as hanging, climbing, running, throwing, leaping, carrying, and jumping. Health is also related to muscular activity; therefore, activities which bring into play all of the fundamental "big muscle "groups in the body should be engaged in regularly. Furthermore, the activity should be of a vigorous nature so that the various organic systems are sufficiently stimulated. Through vigorous muscular activity several beneficial results take place. The trained provides better nourishment to the entire body. The trained hearts slower than the untrained nears it pumps more brood per stroke, with the result that more food is delivered to the cells and there is better removal of waste products.

During exercise the trained heart's speed increases less and has a longer rest period between beats. After exercise it returns to normal much more rapidly. The end result of this state is that the trained individual is able to perform work for a longer period of time, with less expenditure of energy, and much more efficiently, than the untrained individual. This trained condition is necessary to a vigorous and abundant life.

From the time an individual rises in the morning until he goes to bed at night, he is continually in need of vitality, strength, endurance, and stamina to per-from routine tasks, be prepared for emergencies, and lead a vigorous life. Therefore, physical education aids in the development of the trained individual so that he will be better able to perform his routine tasks and live a healthy, interesting, and happy existence.

The motor development objective is concerned with performing physical movement with as little expenditure of energy as possible and in a proficient, graceful, and esthetic manner. This has implications for one's work, play, and anything else which requires physical movement.

The name "motor" is derived from relationship to a nerve or fibre which connects the central nervous system, or a a ganglion, with a muscle. As a consequence of the impulse it transmits, movement results. The impulse it delivers is known as the motor impulse. Effective motor movement is dependent upon a harmonious working together of the muscular and nervous systems.

It results in greater distance between fatigue and peak performance; it is activities which involve such things as running, jumping, dodging, leaping, kicking, bending, twisting, carrying, and throwing; it will enable one to perform his daily work much more efficiently and without reaching the point of being "worn out" so quickly. In physical education activities, the function of efficient body movement, or neuromuscular skill as it is often called, is to provide the individual with the ability to perform with a degree of proficiency. This will result in greater enjoyment of participation.

Most individuals enjoy doing those particular things in which they have acquired a degree of mastery or skill. For example, if a child has mastered the ability to throw a ball consistently to a designated spot and has developed batting and fielding power, he will like to play baseball or softball. If be can swim 25 or 50 yards without tiring and can perform several dives, he will enjoy being in the water. If an adult can consistently serve tennis "aces" he will like tennis; if he can drive a ball 250 yards straight down the fairway, he will like golf; and if he can throw ringers, he will like horseshoes.

A person enjoys doing those things in which he or she excels. Few individuals enjoy participating in activities in which they have little skill. Therefore, it is the objective of physical education to develop in each individual as many physical skills as possible so that interests will be wide and varied. This will not only result in more enjoyment for the participant, but at the same time will allow for better adjustment to group situations. Physical skills are not developed in one lesson. It takes years to acquire co-ordinations, and the most important period for development is during the formative years of a child's growth. The building of co-ordinations starts in childhood, when an individual attempts to synchronize his muscular and nervous systems for such things as creeping, walking, running, and jumping.

A study of kinesiology shows that many muscles of the body are used in even the most simple of co-ordinated movements. Therefore, in order to obtain efficient motor movement or skill in many activities, it is necessary to training early in life and continue into adulthood.

Furthermore, a child does not object to the continual trial-and-error process of achieving success in the performance of physical acts. He dose not object to being observed as an awkward, uncoordinated beginner during the learning period. Most adults, however, are self-conscious when going through the period of learning a physical skill. They do not like to perform if they cannot perform in a creditable manner. The skills they do not acquire in their youth are many times never acquired.

Therefore the physical education profession should try to see that this skill-learning takes place at a time when a person is young and willing and is laying the foundation for adult years. The motor development objective also has important implications for the health and recreational phases of the programme.

The skills that children acquire will determine to a great extent how their leisure time will be spent. One enjoys participating in those activities in which one excels. Therefore if a child excels in swimming, a great deal of his leisure time is going to be spent in a pool, lake, or art the beach. If he excels in tennis, he will be found on the courts on Saturdays, Sundays, and after dinner at night.

There is a marked correlation between juvenile delinquency and lack of constructive leisure-time activity. If we children to spend their leisure moments in a physically wholesome way, we should see that skills are gained in physical education activities.

The mental development objective deals with the accumulation of a body of knowledge and the ability to think and interpret this knowledge. Physical activities must be learned; hence, there is a need for thinking on the part of the intellectual mechanisms with a resulting acquisition of knowledge.

The co-ordinations involved in various movements must be mastered and adapted to the environment in which the individual lives, whether it be in walking, running, or wielding a tennis racquet. In all these movements the child think and co-ordinate his muscular and nervous systems.

The individual should not only learn co-ordinations but should acquire a knowledge of such things as rules, techniques, and strategies involved in physical activities. Basketball can be used as an example. In this sport a person should know such things as the rules, the strategy in offense and defense, the various types of passes, the difference between screening and blocking, and finally the values that are derived from playing in this sport. Techniques which are learned through experience result in knowledge that is also acquired.

For example, a ball travels faster and more accurately if one steps with a pass, and time is saved when the pass is made from the same position in which it is received. Furthermore, a knowledge of followership, leadership, courage, self-reliance, assistance to others, safety, and adaptation to group patterns is very important. Knowledge concerning health should play an important part in the programme.

All individuals should know about their bodies, the importance of sanitation, factors in disease prevention, importance of exercise, need for a well-balanced diet, values of good health attitudes and habits and the community and school agencies which provide health services.

This knowledge will contribute greatly to physical prowess as well as to general health. Through the accumulation of a knowledge of these facts, activities will take on a new meaning and health practices will be associated with definite purposes. This will help each individual to live a healthier and more purposeful life. A store of knowledge will give each individual the proper background for interpreting new situations which confront him from day to day.

Unless there is knowledge to draw from, he will become helpless when called upon to make important decisions. As a result of participation in physical education activities, an individual will be better able to make discriminatory judgments, by which knowledge of values is mentally derived. This means that he has greater power for arriving at a wise decision and that he can better discern right from wrong and the logical from the illogical.

Through his experience in various games and sports, he has developed a sense of values, an alertness, the ability to diagnose a tense situation, the ability to make a decision quickly under highly emotionalized conditions, and the ability to interpret human actions. In physical education activities one also gains insight into human nature.

The various forms of activity in physical education are social experiences which enable a participant to learn about human nature. For all children and youth this is one of the main sources of such knowledge. Here they discover the individual's responsibility to the group, the need for followership and leadership, the need to experience success, and the feeling of "belonging." Here they learn how human beings react to satisfactions and annoyances. Such knowledge contributes to social efficiency and good human relations.

The human relations objective is concerned with helping an individual make personal adjustments, group adjustments, and adjustments as a member of society. Activities in the physical education programme offer one of the best opportunities for making these adjustments, if there is proper leadership. Social action is a result of certain hereditary and derivative tendencies.

There are interests, hungers, desires, ideals, attitudes and emotional drives that are responsible for everything we do. A child wants to play because of his drive for physical activity. A man will steal food because of the hunger drive. America is opposed to totalitarian governments because of its desire for personal freedom. The responses to all these desires, drives, hungers, and the like may be either social or antisocial in nature.

The value of physical education reveals itself when we realize that play activities are one of the oldest and most fundamental drives in human nature. Therefore, by providing the child with a satisfying experience in activities in which he has a natural desire to engage the opportunity is presented to develop desirable social traits. The key is qualified leadership. All human beings should experience success. This factor can be realized through play.

Through successful experience in play activities, a child develops self-confidence and finds happiness in his achievements. Physical education can provide for this successful experience by offering a variety of activities and developing the necessary skills for success in these activities.

An individual who is happy is much more likely to make the right adjustment than the individual who is morbid, sullen, and in an unhappy state of mind. Happiness reflects friendliness, cheerfulness, and a spirit of co-operation, all of which help a person to be content and to conform to the necessary standards which have been established.

Therefore,physical education should instill happiness by guiding children into these activities where this quality will be realized. In a democratic society all individuals should develop a sense of group consciousness and co-operative living. This should be one of the most important objectives of the physical education programme. Whether of not a child will grow up to be a good citizen and contribute to the welfare of society will depend to a great extent upon the training he receives during his youth.

Therefore, in various play activities, the following factors should be stressed:aid for the less-skilled and weaker players,respect for the rights of others, subordination of one's desires to the will of the group, and realization that co-operative living is an essential to the success of society. In other words, the golden rule should be practiced.

The individual should be made to feel that he belongs to the group and has the responsibility of directing his actions in its behalf. The rules of the sportsmanship should be developed and practiced in all activities that are offered in the programme. Such things as courtesy, sympathy, truthfulness, fairness, honesty, respect for authority, and abiding by the rules will help a great deal in the promotion of social efficiency.

The necessity for good leadership and followership should also be stressed as important to the interests of society. The needs and desires which form the basis for people's actions can be controlled through proper training. This training can result in effective citizenship, which is the basis of sound, democratic living.

Effective citizenship is not something that can be developed by artificial stimuli. It is something that is achieved only through activities in which individuals engage in their normal day-to-day routine. Since play activities have such a great attraction for youth, and since it is possible to develop desirable social traits under proper guidance,physical education should realize its responsibility. It should do its part in contributing to good citizenship the basis of our democratic society.

In this chaotic world with its cold wars, hot wars, hydrogen bombs, racial strife, imperialistic aims, human ambitions, and class struggles, human relations are more and more important to personal, group, and world peace. Only through a better understanding of one's fellow man, will it be possible to build a peaceful and democratic world.

Good Administration

Good administration is an essential in the fields of school health and physical education if the goals which have been set for these professors are to be realized. There must be harmony encouraged among the various members of the staff, adequate facilities provided, the programme planned and continually re-evaluated, a public relations plan established, leadership provided, and many other essentials and details attended to with dispatch if the objectives are to be achie ved.The administrator is a key person.

The administrator sets the pace. The administrator provides the leadership. If this individual does not assume the responsibilities which go with such a position, there will be apathy and indifference all along the line and consequently the aims or which the professions exist will not be realized.

Administrators must continually keep in mind the goals towards which they are working. With these in mind they should gear their staff relationships, programmes, and other factors in a way which will be must efficient and productive from the standpoint of realizing such goals.

Administrators frequently have both the areas of health and physical education within their administrative division. This affords opportunity to promote the kind of co-operation that is needed to achieve the aims of each. One cannot be promoted at the expense of the other. One cannot be recognized as being more important than the other. If such is the practice, progress place that each area has in the total picture.

All administrative policies must preserve this balance. If the administrators have only one of these specialized areas within their division, this should not limit their relationship with the other. Both areas are closely allied and it is very important that they work closely together. Administrators will determine in large measure whether or not this becomes a reality. The administrator should be familiar with the role of professional organizations in his work. He should realize that these associations promote professional ethics, scholarship, leadership, and high educational standards. .

Psychological Environment

An appropriate environment for a quality physical education program enables and encourages all students to discover new concepts, skills, and abilities through movement experiences and other aspects of the physical education program. The atmosphere should be a nonthreatening one in which every student feels that to risk trying something new is safe physically, emotionally, and sccially. Emphasis should be placed throughout on the development of movement skills, fitness and wellness, self-confidence, and social skills.

Because of the complexities of human growth and development and individual and cultural differences among students, a comprehensive physical education program should include a wide variety of movement experiences and teaching-learning strategies. All students should have the opportunity to be successful.

Throughout, the student must experience a climate of respect -for oneself, for others, and for physical education generally, especially when students are being directed in attempts to refine skills or are being disciplined. Disciplinary procedures should be appropriate to the infraction, and the assignment of physical exercise should not be used as punishment. To do so will not instill in the student a love of physical activity.

Another important aspect of the psychological environment is an emphasis on accepting and celebrating ethnic and cultural diversity, one of the most challenging issues in education. Physical education offers unique opportunities to bring students together in nonthreatening ways that emphasize fairness and cooperation.

The atmosphere should be a nonthreatening one in which every student feels that to risk trying something new is safe physically, emotionally, and socially.. taught the personal and social skills, values, and attitudes needed for effective, positive social interaction. Disparaging remarks about an individual's disabilities, ethnicity, gender, native language, race, religion, or sexual orientation should not be tolerated.

The physical education program must comply fully with all federal and state mandates. Appropriate instruction in physical education for culturally diverse populations may require special teaching skills and a focus on students ' unique needs. Teachers must avoid cultural or gender biases and refrain from stereotyping students. Students from different cultures may respond differently to directions from the teacher, praise and acknowledgment from others, perceived expectations, and physical interaction. Teachers should learn to recognize and understand the influence of their students cultural heritage and learn to accommodate diversity while achieving the goals of the physical education curriculum.

Although the school is the primary learning environment for physical education, the home and community also play significant roles. Only through the cooperation of the school, the home, and the community can students become fully prepared for lifelong participation in physical activity and effective social interaction. The school site can become a focus for cooperation among families and outside support systems.

Designating the school as the contact point provides families with more opportunities to receive services that benefit the child's health and development. For example, interaction of school and family can help to promote an acceptance of physically active and healthier, happier, more productive life-styles throughout the community.

Schools can establish centres for wellness that provide assessment of physical well-being, individual counselling, and a variety of fitness activities. They can also involve families in other extracurricular activities at the school site and coordinate school and community recreational programs.

The community, working closely with the school, can play an active role in promoting fitness and wellness by providing opportunities for physical activity for families and individuals. Through participation in a variety of physical activities at school, students will be better prepared to take advantage of opportunities for physical activity provided in the home or in the community.

In Kindergarten, at the elementary level the physical education curriculum needs to focus on basic skills by having students participate in many types of age-appropriate activities. As their skills develop, students can begin to understand that correct practice will result in improved learning and development of competency.

In the upper elementary grades, students can become involved in activities that will assist in their own learning and help them begin to appreciate individual differences in their peers.

At the middle school level, students can benefit from experiences that will assist them in evaluating and measuring their own performance. They can begin to recognize and develop practice schedules for different skills appropriate to their varying abilities. They can also be involved in activities in which they design schedules with and give appropriate feedback to their peers. Eventually, students can apply these concepts to new skills and thus transfer learning.

At the high school level, students may design their own learning schedules based on their own choice of activities. Throughout, it is important for planners and instructors to become aware of the total experience of a comprehensive system across age groups. Even during the early stages, a well-planned physical education program takes account of the long-term goals.

Teachers of primary students are aware, for example, that students are moving toward the ultimate goal of making independent choices about physical activity in their teenage years. In addition, the element of pleasure in physical activity and an emphasis on pleasurable play should be a continual focus of physical education.

Children at this stage are solo learners. They focus primarily on moving within space, including the general space around them and their own personal space. Nonlocomotor skills include how the body moves on its axis, and locomotor skills include moving in general space.

Once the children are able to move effectively in their space, they focus on objects -for example, equipment, supplies, and materials. They also learn about and interpret their environment through play. They should move in a safe environment that helps them look forward to positive experiences in physical education.

At this stage children can be guided to move in their environment for the sheer enjoyment of exploring space and controlling their bodies. They learn basic movement skills, including creeping, crawling, walking, hopping, and galloping on the preferred foot, playing rhythmic games and song games, and participating in circle or partner walks and marches.

Nonlocomotor movement experiences include balancing, bending and stretching, twisting and turning, beating and shaking, tensing and relaxing, pushing and pulling, rising and falling, and participating in rhythmic and play activities that require those movements. Children in kindergarten also learn the concept of static stability by experiencing various balances that position the center of gravity over the base of support. They learn that the body is in a stable, balanced position when the center of gravity is directly over the base of support and that improvement occurs when a skill is practiced many times.

Object manipulation includes opportunities to manipulate and play with a wide variety of objects: lightweight balls, soft objects, beanbags, ribbons, hoops, and such student-made objects as sock balls, for example. At this stage students also perform free exploratory movement to rhythmic or musical accompaniment that is prerecorded or provided by the teacher or other students. The kindergarten experience begins with the expansion of knowledge of the physical self through identification of body parts -both external (e.g., arms, legs, head, and facial features) and internal (e.g., heart and lungs).

Physical Education Guidelines

Basically ego-oriented, children in kindergarten tend to play alone in their own space. They are focused on themselves in the present. At this stage children can be guided to move in their environment for the sheer enjoyment of exploring space and controlling their bodies. However, they also begin to recognize the concept of self and others; acknowledge that others may occupy their space; learn to move about in their space without interfering with others; and begin to learn to take turns and share in interaction with others. Children at this stage generally do not understand the purpose of rules but will follow rules delivered by adults. In Kindergarten the stages of children's growth is divided into twelve grades:

Grade One

Students at this stage expand their movement skills to include qualities of space and time by learning to move in different directions at varying speeds. They explore a variety of movements, such as high-low and fast-slow. They also learn to recognize the element of time in movement -for example, how long it takes to move from one place to another and how long it takes an object to travel from one place to another.

Through movement experiences first graders develop an awareness of the concepts of space, time, and effort. These experiences should include many opportunities for children to feel the joy that results from having the ability and freedom to explore, discover, and express themselves through movement.

As they continue motor learning, first graders accept challenges to move through space with the added dimensions of time and effort, such as fast-slow and strong-weak. Direction in movement is introduced along with basic eye-hand and eye-foot manipulative skills. Locomotor activities include hopping on the nonpreferred foot; galloping on the nonpreferred foot; and marching, sliding, and performing other patterns according to specific rhythms.

Nonlocomotor movements include symmetrical and asymmetrical balances, lifting and carrying, starting and stopping, swinging, swaying, curling, and stationary dodging. Students make deliberate moves in specified directions. They learn the biomechanical principle of dynamic stability. That is, balance is inherent in all movement, and individuals can increase their static stability by widening their base of support and lowering their center of gravity.

They also learn that movement begins when their center of gravity moves to the edge of their base of support, their center of gravity is raised, and their base of support is narrowed. For example, a student is running, comes to a stop to maintain balance, and resumes running. Students begin to manipulate objects with purposeful movement and learn to roll, toss underhand, bounce with two hands, retrieve, stationary-kick, and strike with the hand various objects that are safe and nonthreatening. Simple dances in columns and circles and basic partner dances are appropriate at this level.

Although the child's movement becomes more purposeful and performance more deliberate, the instructor should encourage interest in the performance of an activity rather than any particular level of achievement. Especially at the beginning of the year, the physical education program should include familiar and enjoyable games and activities that allow for each child's full participation.

First graders learn about the body's need for oxygen and food as fuel to supply the body with energy. They also learn about the role of the circulatory system in moving oxygenated blood to the muscles. They reflect on how their bodies feel as they experiment with different types of movement -for example, differing periods of time and types of space. The relationship of nutrition and exercise to physical strength and energy should be introduced at this level.

Children at this stage begin to form a personal body image through comparison with others. They learn that the body undergoes marked changes in height and weight and that those changes influence the movement and coordination of body parts.

First graders participate in parallel play with other students and tend to be more involved in individual activities than in interaction with others. They continue to learn in groups but participate as individuals.

Grade Two

At this stage students explore movement patterns with a partner to define movement in relation to another person, shape, or group. They learn by continuing to experience a variety of modalities, including kinesthetic learning. Since the students are highly flexible in interacting with partners, activities should encourage changes of partners. In the application of rules, fairness at this stage is flexible, and children are likely to make up their own rules as they play together.

Total physical response with the entire body -occurs in motor movement as the student learns to define movement in relation to another person, shape, group, or group shape. Locomotor patterns include leaping and skipping, dancing with a partner, and dancing in a double circle. Nonlocomotor movements include dynamic balancing, dodging while moving, pantomiming, and mirror moving.

As students begin to play in partnerships, simple dances for couples, such as the Children's Polka, are appropriate movement and apply laws of motion at higher grade levels, students learn to describe movement and differentiate among speed, velocity, and acceleration. With partners second graders are able to compare various speeds and velocities. For example, students can talk about how fast they can run or walk and the difference between running and walking and other modes of locomotion.

Manipulative skills include catching a rolled ball; throwing and catching after one bounce (solo and with a partner); and kicking a stationary ball in a variety of ways. In addition to physical practice, students at this level should be encouraged to begin to use visualization and mental practice to reinforce learning.

The study of exercise physiology considers how the heart and lungs work as partners in cardiorespiratory health. In pairs students monitor the pulse at rest, during exercise, and after exercise. As they participate in movement that accelerates breathing and pulse rate, they learn the concept of the body's need for exercise to accelerate breathing and pulse rates on a regular basis. Nutrition, with a focus on foods healthy for the heart, is another factor in developing students ' knowledge and skills related to cardiorespiratory health.

Growth rates vary during this stage. As the children's awareness of others increases, they are able increasingly to see themselves in relation to others. They are also able to recognize and appreciate their own positive and negative feelings and those of others.

In grade two children learn more about relationships between themselves and others. They move from the sense of self in isolation and begin to embrace the concept of we and partners .This is also a time when children's growing awareness of others can help to promote knowledge of individual differences and different cultures. That can be the springboard, in turn, for encouraging children to accept and appreciate differences in others. The children are able to celebrate the successes of others and begin to recognize specific activities that contribute to feelings of joy and movement experiences that rely on cooperation. They consistently practice sharing and caring skills when playing with partners in movement activities and reinforce one another by giving and receiving encouragement.

Grade Three

Reacting and responding to others take precedence at this stage. By now students have a self-image strong enough to tolerate differences in how others react to them and are better able to make well-defined combinations of movements. Groups should never number more than five, the number that provides everyone with many turns and allows for natural leaders and followers to emerge.

Students motor ability increases as they gain greater control. They begin to develop a concept of the order of a sequence in movement and willingly experiment with and explore alternative movements. Third graders learn a variety of rhythmic patterns and grade-appropriate dances, using specific movement patterns, such as step-hop, step-swing, and two-step. Nonlocomotor skill development focuses on balance, including the use of apparatuses, inverted balances, balance on various body parts, and partner balances.

Students are able to describe muscular movement as the internal force that causes the body to change from a stationary to a moving object. They can also describe gravity, friction, and muscular movements as the external forces that cause the body to stop. They learn that specific types of movement provide benefits not only in developing skills but also in developing and maintaining health fitness. Striking skills, such as dribbling and volleying, continue to be refined.

Students are also able to discriminate among cues, adjust to cues, and determine appropriate movements for specific situations. This stage foreshadows the marked physical changes that will take place in later childhood. The exercise physiology experience for grade three includes an emphasis on the importance of aerobic exercise for cardiorespiratory health, including the principles of warming up before exercising and cooling down afterward.

In keeping with the grade-level emphasis on continuity and change, students participate in warm-up exercises to change the body to a readiness state for more vigorous exercise. In extended periods of aerobic activity, they also experience continuity of effort in cardiorespiratory conditioning. A third health-fitness component, flexibility, is emphasized during the warm-up and cooling-down phases.

Third graders begin to express themselves by creating new movement patterns involving time, space, and flow. They continue to celebrate successes and identify activities contributing to feelings of joy through active play.

Students learn through play to handle individual responsibilities and resolve personal differences, becoming more capable of working together for a common goal as they grow in their ability to cooperate and take turns. The teacher should encourage the formation of groups of mixed gender during structured sessions because at this level boys and girls tend to separate for free play.

During this stage students begin to gain respect for other classmates and for the property of others, understand different types of play, and assist each other by practicing with a partner the rules of fair play. They learn to listen to each other and to react and respond appropriately.

Grade Four

Fourth graders are at a stage between childhood and youth during which they are growing in definite patterns. Eye-hand coordination is improved, and fine-motor activities are becoming more skillful. In addition, the greatest gain in strength begins at this stage. Students have mastered many locomotor and nonlocomotor skills and are able to manipulate objects in a variety of ways. They can create a game, for example, when they are given an object and encouraged to play.

Physiologically, while they are standing, their center of gravity is still located in the midsection of the body, making balance and manipulation of objects a challenge. Fourth graders are likely to test rules during play and challenge how rules apply to them. Further, they tend to regard rules as rigid and prescriptive. When exceptions to the rules have to be made, the logic and rationale of the rules should be emphasized.

In motor development students at this level are able to focus on refining their skills in comparison with proficiency standards. They begin to use space and distance appropriately as they progress toward accuracy in throwing, catching, manipulating the body in space, and striking with body parts and objects -for example, volleying and dribbling a basketball with the hands and moving a soccer ball with the feet.

They also learn about the concepts of projection -for example, applying greater force to an object to make it travel farther and knowing how to generate force by maintaining firm contact with the ground when the object is released. Rhythmic activities include specific dances that may be related to the history -social science curriculum, such as dances appropriate to specific regions, ethnic groups, and cultures.

Students also learn that there are many ways to learn and practice movement skills and that a practice session can be conducted in a variety of ways. Whole practice involves learning an entire sequence of movements that combine into a complex skill pattern; partial practice involves concentrating on one fundamental movement.

Some skills may be introduced whole, learned in parts, and then practiced whole. Fitness-conditioning activities focus on various types of health-fitness exercises and many ways to combine those exercises into an exercise program. Another focus is on how physical exercise conditions the heart, lungs, and muscles.

Students learn to differentiate between aerobic exercises that provide cardiorespiratory benefits and those that do not. They also learn about the importance of muscular endurance and strength as components of fitness. The role of nutrients in forming body composition and providing the energy needed to sustain physical movement should also be emphasized.

At this level students are ready to cope with success and failure and are more perceptive and accepting of similarities and differences. This is also a time for developing, in the individual and in the group, wholesome attitudes toward victory and defeat. Appreciation of different styles of movement and the uniqueness of movement in various cultures begins to occur. Thus, fourth graders appreciate a sense of personal uniqueness in movement and become aware of the similarities and differences between themselves and others.

Fourth graders are ready to take the initiative within the group and demonstrate leadership as well as learn to be a good follower. This level is appropriate for the introduction of more complex games that challenge and increase performance abilities and enhance social skills. Fourth graders are able to cooperate with a partner in using equipment and helping one another improve object manipulation skills.

Working together as part of large groups, they begin to appreciate personal differences and value the rights of others. They want to follow rules; thus, they need to learn to cope with conflicts and disputes by practicing conflict-resolution skills. While considering diversity in California, students observe that local demographics and geography influence the type of physical activities and recreational opportunities available within a given area - for example, skiing in the mountains and swimming and surfing at the ocean. Students also consider multicultural influences on the evolution of games and the varieties of game rules in different geographical areas.

GRADE FIVE

At this level students continue to manipulate a variety of objects according to more specific goals. Now accuracy and speed, with a focus on targets, become important. Eye-hand, eye-foot; and other forms of coordination begin to come together.

Fifth graders try continually to improve their motor skills, celebrate their successes and achievements, and take pride in individual excellence. Groups are expanded to include more than five students, and cooperative learning parallels that of other academic subjects. At this level the concept of fairness is emphasized. Students may be willing to change rules in order to achieve fairness for all.

At this stage specific body types are more efficient in certain movements, skills, and activities as body size and strength increase steadily. As students continue to improve in motor performance, they become more proficient in basic skills, such as running, jumping, and throwing. The ten-year-old begins to concentrate on the development of selective motor skills.

Fifth-grade students manipulate objects through space with accuracy and with the added element of speed. As they practice for skill and accuracy, students learn that the desired expectation determines the type of practice needed to achieve that goal. One type of practice may be to concentrate on improving speed, another on improving accuracy, and still another on improving both.

In the application of Newton's second law, students experiment in throwing different sizes of balls (golf ball, shot, softball), discovering that smaller objects will travel farther than heavier objects when the same amount of force is used. When speed is the objective, they learn to use a flat trajectory. They learn that to catch an object, they must increase (1) the distance through which the object moves after contact; or (2) the size of the area that absorbs the force of the object.

In grade five students examine the role of the circulatory system and its relationship to overall health.They are taught to develop strength and flexibility, including the interaction of strength and flexibility with the ability to perform forceful movements or manipulate objects with force. Further, they are taught how to maintain a healthy body by balancing food intake with physical activity (calories consumed and calories expended) and regulating the ratio of lean to fat body tissue.

Students at this stage learn to establish goals and select the practice techniques appropriate to the most immediate goals. They play gamelike activities in which the use of more than two skills to achieve objectives in the game is emphasized.

Experiencing individual satisfaction increases at this stage as a motivational factor for future participation in a variety of activities. Increasingly, fifth-graders are able to use the body in movement to communicate feelings and to appreciate the aesthetic aspects of physical performance and the pleasure of achieving goals they have set for themselves.

Fifth graders thrive in small-group activity in which three to five students interact in cooperative play. They assume increasingly complex roles in cooperative activities; begin to develop an awareness of individual differences related to gender, cultural heritage, ethnicity, and physical ability; and appreciate the positive aspects of diversity.

Social and game patterns include one against two, two against three, and two against two in activities such as goaltending. Students are beginning to recognize offensive and defensive play and understand that strategy is a skill to be developed within the context of play and games. Fifth graders know how to apply rules and demonstrate a sense of fairness in games and activities. Contemporary music and dance are popular. The California Raisin Dance and the Electric Slide, for example, can be modified to create more complex dance patterns.

Grade Six

Students at this stage are able to combine various skills in cooperative activities and give appropriate feedback to others. More independent in thought and action than younger students, they are also more likely to seek out new challenges in individual and group activities. Despite their desire for independence, however, sixth graders are likely to be genuinely interested in helping others. Because their interest in team play and organized games is strong, learning experiences can focus on developing the skills required for cooperative effort toward a common goal.

Students at this level are ready to combine skills for practice in lead-up games (a team, individual, or dual activity leading to an organized sport). These activities facilitate the learning of physical skills while allowing for cooperative effort. A unit should be included in sixth grade on cooperative games that can be used as lead-up games for more traditional sports.

Juggling, unicycling, pogo-stick activities, bowling, foot-bag skill games, and throwing activities add variety and challenge as students improve their eye-hand and eye-foot coordination. This is also an appropriate time to add tumbling to previously learned stunts. Students learn concepts related to Newton's third law. That is, when struck, an object will rebound in the opposite direction with the same amount of force with which it is hit. The harder an object is hit, the greater will be the force that causes the object to rebound in the opposite direction.

A child's development, which is influenced by heredity, hormones, nutrition, and exercise, is also influenced by cultural expectations and gender differences. Students should understand that the achievement of certain levels of physical skill is dependent on all of these factors and that they should accept individual differences.

Sixth graders are beginning to understand the purpose of each health-fitness component and the interrelatedness of all the fitness components in the development and maintenance of optimum health. Special emphasis should be given to the interaction of the circulatory and respiratory systems in conditioning for health fitness.

Students at this stage are able to recognize stylistic differences in performance, develop a more realistic self-image, and form collective attitudes as members of a group. They also begin to value looking good more than ever before as they become more aware of the varying levels of physical development within their peer group.

Despite the physiological differences that occur at this age, students are generally willing to work cooperatively toward a common goal because desire for recognition within the group is strong. The physical education experience should foster in each student a sense of acceptance and belonging and of being valued within the group or on a team.

During lead-up games students at this level begin to recognize the validity of rule application and to accept that fairness applies to all. The grouping patterns for games can increase in size to six players. In keeping with the grade six history-social science focus on ancient civilizations, it is appropriate to introduce students to tribal dances and ethnic dances of contemporary or ancient cultures. Examples include the Pata Pata from South Africa, the Hora from Israel, and the High Life from Ghana.

As students work in cooperative groups, they learn to provide one another with feedback and support in skill execution. They learn through experimentation that specific, positive, corrective feedback improves skill development more rapidly than general, negative, or neutral feedback and that the more promptly feedback is given after performance, the more meaningful the feedback is.

Cooperation includes interacting with opponents in competitive activities to facilitate mutual development of skills. Sixth graders can accept and respect the performance of others, regardless of ability level, and are able to interact positively with others to develop friendships and participate in peer coaching activities with a partner.

Grade Seven

A well-planned physical education program takes into account the importance of the transition from sixth to eighth grade and the rapid physical, social, and emotional changes occurring at this level. Students are beginning to look for a sense of belonging, community, peer group, and team even as they are gaining more confidence in individual activities.

They have an eagerness to test themselves, both individually and in groups. This is an appropriate time to introduce individual risk taking and individual sports rather than focus exclusively on team sports.

Students at this stage tend to enjoy risk-related activities. Unless the school curriculum provides such activities in a safe environment, the students are likely to pursue the activities on their own without supervision. Appropriate activities include aquatics; combatives (e.g., self-defence and fencing); tumbling; gymnastics; individual and dual sports; and outdoor education, such as adventure-based activities and orienteering.

Specific adventure-based activities might include problem-solving exercises in which students work in small groups to solve physical challenges; trust falls (the student falls backward into the arms of partners); low-rope activities, such as balancing on a log suspended above the ground; high-rope activities in which students are involved in rappelling or rock climbing; and rollerskating, skateboarding, and cycling. The tumbling unit introduced in grade six can be extended at this level to include apparatus for gymnastics and rhythmic gymnastics.

Seventh graders should learn more about the principles of spin and rebound. Spin results when force is applied off the center of an object. Students should become familiar with and begin to experiment with spins of various types: counter clockwise, clockwise, backspin, and topspin. They should learn how spin can be used to gain strategic advantage by players who understand how to apply it.

Dance should include folk dances and other dances from cultures around the world to help students develop greater understanding and acceptance of their own heritage and that of others. As for motor learning, students at this level should understand that performance is measurable in terms of technique, accuracy, distance, and speed. They should be able to chart their own motor skill development-in specific activities and events.

Seventh graders are also able to understand the interrelationship of the health-fitness components in the development of optimum health and thus to select specific exercises for each component. This is an appropriate time to introduce the FIT guidelines for physical exercise, which are the appropriate frequency, intensity, and time required for benefits to be accrued in each health-fitness component. Students should learn the principles of overload, progression, and specificity in physical conditioning.

Students ' growth rates vary considerably during this period of development. Many experience their most rapid growth, and an increasing number show signs of puberty. All need to be aware that they must continue strenuous activity to maintain strength, speed, and endurance as their bodies change.

They should study the impact of such factors as exercise, relaxation, nutrition, stress, and substance abuse on the body's ability to participate in physical exercise and on general well-being. Screening for posture deviation is required of all seventh graders, and parents must be notified when further examination is recommended.

The seventh grader is entering a time when he or she is more likely than ever before to take on new challenges, solve new problems, and be willing to take new risks. Risk taking involves new challenges and learning opportunities -trying out new equipment and new ways to use old equipment. Risk taking is attractive to students both alone and with others.

They should be given a variety of opportunities to experience controlled risks through such activities as planned outdoor adventure activities and ropes courses. Students are also more likely to accept the challenge of setting personal goals for improvement related to health fitness and performance skills.

Seventh graders are increasingly able to meet challenges, solve problems, and resolve conflicts within a group. They are more likely to express an appreciation for cooperation and fair play as they adhere to group rules. This is also a time when students develop confidence to overcome anxieties associated with attempting something new, making new friends, and beginning to accept their own limitations.

Grade Eight

Students should be encouraged to continue participation in group activities because all aspects of the personal development of eighth graders, both physical and mental, are still evolving.

By the end of the eighth grade, students should have experienced a wide variety of activities. Now they can begin to see relationships among sports skills. For example, they may learn the underhand pitch for softball in one unit and transfer that skill to the underhand serve in volleyball and the serve in badminton. They should also be encouraged to understand that in certain situations transfer of learning can have a negative effect, such as learning the forehand drive in tennis and then applying it to the forehand drive in badminton.

A comparison of the offensive and defensive techniques used in team sports should be offered to help eighth graders learn the basic principles of strategy. In addition, students should have the opportunity to continue in a tumbling/gymnastics unit and a dance unit. Group dances, such as square, round, and contemporary line dances with directional changes requiring group cooperation, are appropriate. In eighth grade students learn the principles of rotation.

That is, to rotate an object, one must apply torque. They also learn that the closer the mass is to the axis, the greater the rotary velocity will be. Eighth graders have many opportunities to experiment with these concepts, particularly during the gymnastics unit. Students learn that growth in height and weight alters the mechanical nature of performance and that motor performance is related to all measures of maturity (chronological, anatomical, and physiological).

Eighth graders are able to begin to design personal plans for a healthy lifestyle. Each student's plan should include exercises that take into account the FIT guidelines taught in grade seven and the principles of training. The importance of appropriate intensity in exercising should be emphasized as students learn to calculate their individual target heart rate for exercise and to understand the importance of cardiorespiratory conditioning. They should also be able to distinguish the health-related fitness components of cardiorespiratory endurance, muscular strength and endurance, flexibility, and body composition.

By eighth grade students should have developed skills needed to reduce stress. Their higher level of motor achievement provides a basis for establishing new personal goals that they can realistically attain. Students are able to accept responsibility for their behaviour and resolve individual and group conflicts. They are mature enough to recognize the difference between ethical and unethical behaviour and appreciate the importance of fair play, cooperation, and competition in team games, activities, and sports.

They are also capable of playing on teams, making decisions, and solving problems associated with physical activities. Team games and team sports are of great interest and value to eighth graders of both genders because they help satisfy the students ' need to feel a sense of belonging to a group.

The team-sports units should include the history, rules, and strategy of each sport. By this time students should understand that the rules are fair to all participants and allow for safe participation. They should also begin to generalize and understand that infringements of the rules involving other people are fouls; that infringements involving space, equipment, or time are violations; and that it is through the manipulation and understanding of the rules that strategies develop.

Group affiliation assumes added importance at this level, with emphasis being placed on team participation, roles of group members, group loyalty, and the identification of ethical and unethical behaviour in group activities.

Students begin to think of themselves as members of a team and learn to cooperate rather than dominate other team members in team and dual sports. They learn to identify and apply specific criteria for successful team participation and to lead and follow by sharing leadership positions.

Grade Nine

This is a stage at which students are able to synthesize much of what they have learned in the earlier grades, including knowledge of human growth, development, and physiology. Individuals are able to coalesce as a team and focus on the needs and contributions of other team members beyond themselves. Affiliation, a feeling of being connected and involved, is of primary importance to ninth graders.

Students develop a willingness to acknowledge and respect stylistic differences in performance. The ninth-grade physical education program should encourage students to gain an appreciation of others ' achievements, no matter how large or small, and to expand their ability to adapt to the needs of the group and demonstrate fairness toward all.

The major emphases of study in the ninth grade are fitness, team sports, gymnastics, and aquatics. In learning about fitness, the students become familiar with new concepts related to the physiology of exercise; become knowledgeable consumers in relation to fitness; and experience a wide variety of exercises for flexibility, muscular strength and endurance, and cardiorespiratory endurance.

In team sports ninth graders should be encouraged to select a sport in which to specialize; learn the history, rules, and strategies of the sport; and become proficient in the appropriate skills. The gymnastics unit should be an extension of the earlier tumbling and gymnastics classes. Here, too, students should be encouraged to select an event in which to specialize. For those students who already demonstrate proficiency in swimming, classes in water polo, skin diving, or advanced swimming can be offered.

During an aquatics unit the students should learn the biomechanical principle of buoyancy. That is, to move efficiently through water, they must streamline their bodies to reduce the effect of drag. In addition, the swimmer's size, shape, surface, and speed of movement are factors affecting performance in swimming.

In grade nine the student is expected to develop an in-depth understanding of the components of total health fitness in a unit that emphasizes the physiological, psychological, and social benefits of a healthy, active lifestyle. Students should also begin to identify preferences for types of physical activity that can be pursued over the long term for fitness and recreation, including individual, dual, or team sports.

Ninth graders should be able to explain the social, personal, and health benefits of developing skills in sports, games, and dance. They should be able to describe the aesthetic qualities of movement; feel good as they move efficiently and effectively; and develop the ability to evaluate personal needs, interests, and capacities that contribute to their movement choices.

In physical education experiences the ninth grader should demonstrate patterns of behaviour that reflect sound mental and emotional health, positive self-image, and acceptance of the total self. To help students achieve self-realization through physical activity, the physical education instructor should guide the student's choice of fitness programs and activities to ensure a healthy lifestyle throughout life. Each student should set personal goals for health and fitness, including goals for improving health through physical exercise.

Ninth graders have the capacity to demonstrate mature teamwork by successfully resolving conflicts within the group. They should learn to cooperate in teamwork and in competition, analyze situations, find solutions to problems, obey rules, work for delayed rewards, and persevere toward a goal.

The ninth grader is becoming increasingly more interested in sports as both participant and spectator. This increased interest is associated with several factors in addition to physical conditioning.

Grade Ten

Students at this stage are capable of choosing the physical activities they want to pursue. They are more able to generalize from previous experiences and to apply biomechanical principles to the analysis of a variety of movement skills. A well-planned physical education program will offer students a wide variety of opportunities. It will focus on individual or team sports of choice, dance, and personal defence, among other activities. The five emphases of study for the tenth grade are individual and dual sports, outdoor education, combatives, dance, and analysis of movement. The individual or dual sport may be of the student's own choosing and may include such outdoor activities as orienteering, rock climbing, backpacking, and skiing.

A personal defence class meets the combatives requirement and teaches students to avoid dangerous situations while preparing to defend themselves. The dance unit can be an extension of units taught at earlier grade levels. It can also be an elective that allows students to specialize in a specific type of dance at an intermediate or advanced level.

The analysis-of-movement class should conclude grade ten whenever possible. Reviewing what they have learned throughout the kindergarten through grade ten physical education curriculum, students should explore the reasons for physical education being taught in school, including the relationship between physical education and personal and social development. This class should also prepare students to be informed consumers in physical and recreational activities they plan to pursue outside of school.

By the end of this unit, students should have developed a lifetime plan for physical fitness and activity. At this grade level students demonstrate improved performance, in part because their perceptual feedback has improved. They have acquired skills that are basic to efficient movement. In addition, they should have acquired a high level of physical fitness.

They should be able to analyze the physiological and mechanical principles involved in human movement and make adjustments in physical exercise to achieve personal goals for fitness or motor performance or both.

The application of the principles of levers to movement should be introduced in tenth grade. The human skeletal system is made up primarily of third-class levers. Because the force arm (muscle) for human beings cannot be lengthened, the students should learn that in order to increase the force at impact with an object, they must strengthen the muscle or lengthen the striking element to increase the force.

Students can apply these concepts in activities such as golf (by using a longer shaft when driving) and tennis (by straightening the arm at the moment of impact in the serve).

The awareness tenth graders have of the importance of commitment and dedication in physical education contributes to their desire to pursue excellence in a variety of ways -socially, emotionally, and intellectually. The tenth-grade physical education curriculum should emphasize that while learning any new skill, individuals go through three stages of learning:

(1) the cognitive phase;

(2) the practice phase; and

(3) the automatic phase, in which skills can be performed without concentrated attention.

Although moving through this cycle takes time, students at the high school level are mature enough to reach the automatic phase in selected skills.

Tenth-grade students should be encouraged to evaluate the potential benefits and risks of available exercise programs in the school and the community and the cost-effectiveness of exercise programs offered to students as consumers.

Each student should plan a personal exercise program that is physiologically sound and appropriate to his or her needs, interests, level of ability; and goals for health fitness.

Grades Eleven and Twelve

Students at this level continue to specialize in activities of their own choosing. In addition, they can pursue excellence in the activities they choose, following a specific regimen and honing specific skills.They are able to develop a personalized plan for lifetime fitness by assessing personal needs, interests, abilities, and opportunities in the area of fitness and by selecting activities that contribute to the achievement of personal fitness goals.

They can also focus on combatives; outdoor education; aquatics; team sports and individual and dual sports of choice; tumbling; gymnastics; and dance. They can apply knowledge, skills, and attitudes acquired in physical education experiences from kindergarten through grade twelve to become proficient in one or more activities that lead to achieving personal goals for lifetime fitness. Schools should be encouraged to be creative in developing their physical education electives for these grade levels.

By the eleventh and twelfth grades, students are prepared to focus on the activities they plan to pursue after graduation from high school. They are able to explain why an individual's pursuit of excellence in any arena is an evolving process requiring commitment, courage, confidence, initiative, and perseverance. They have learned that self-expression through physical activity is of great value in developing and maintaining the healthy mind and body needed to excel in life.

Students should be encouraged to select a variety of activities that correspond to their personal needs, interests, and capacities. They should also be encouraged to reassess their changing needs and interests continually as they grow and mature.

Students should be encouraged to select activities in which they will continue to specialize. Therefore, the biomechanical principles they study should be directly related to the activities they select. The students should also be encouraged to apply their knowledge of exercise physiology in planning and pursuing life-styles conducive to maintaining optimum health.

The senior high school student is at a stage where he or she can develop an increased interest in selecting activities in accordance with personal body type and capacities. By the eleventh grade students should have learned to evaluate personal performance in a variety of activities.

By the eleventh and twelfth grades, students are prepared to focus on the activities they plan to pursue for recreation or a career after graduation from high school. Elective units in a wide range of activities should last for a sufficient period of time. Students who complete these classes should be well prepared to continue the activity on their own. An individual's pursuit of excellence in any arena is an evolving process requiring commitment, courage, confidence, initiative, and perseverance.

Students should be encouraged to work in small groups to provide one another with specific positive/ corrective feedback so that individual excellence can be achieved. They should apply social skills acquired in physical education activities in preschool through grade twelve to enhance their own experience and the experience of others with whom they are involved in physical and social activities. They should also be encouraged to support and participate in community organizations that promote health and fitness by providing lifelong recreational opportunities for people of all ages.

3

Games from Ancient to Modern Periods

A game is a recreational activity involving one or more players, defined by a) a goal that the players try to reach, and b) some set of rules that determines what the players can do. Games are played primarily for entertainment or enjoyment. Games can involve one player acting alone, but more often involve competition among two or more players. Taking an action that falls outside the rules generally constitutes a foul or cheating. All through human history, people have played games to entertain themselves and others, and there is an enormous variety of games types.

Many technical fields are often applied to the study of games, including probability, statistics, economics, ethnomathematics, and game theory.

Many of the games people played a long time ago, we still play today. Other games have now been completely forgotten. Most of them are fun to play, though.

Ball games have been known for thousands of years. People made balls out of leather stuffed with cloth scraps or wool, sewn together with leather thongs or string (like a football today). There are pictures of both boys and girls throwing balls to one another, and of boys in classical Athens playing a game like field hockey with curved sticks and a ball. (Unfortunately we don't know the rules). In this picture you can see a girl juggling three balls, on a vase from Athens in the 400's BC.

By this time, and possibly much earlier, people also played marbles, with small balls made out of clay (the crummy ones) and out of real marble (the good ones). (Glass marbles were not invented until much later. It is still possible, though not easy, to buy clay marbles, but we have not found a source for stone ones). Again we don't know the rules. But probably they played the same basic games of marbles that we know today: one version where you take turns tossing the marbles at a goal (another marble, a hole, or a wall), and another version where you take turns shooting the marbles within a circle drawn in the dirt, trying to get them out of the circle.

Another type of game was *played with wooden hoops and sticks,* either tossing the hoop up in the air and trying to keep it up in the air with the sticks (rather like a hula hoop), or rolling the hoop along the ground pushing it with the stick.

Many very simple games are also very old, like *running races and playing tag, or competing to see who can jump the highest or the farthest.* They also played hopscotch, which seems to have started out as a training exercise for the Roman army.

The Egyptians, Greeks, and Romans were also very fond of *board games* like backgammon and checkers. Archaeologists often find paving stones in houses and in public buildings and sidewalks which have had little hollows carved out of them to place stones in, to play board games. The hollows are made in different patterns for different games. Again we don't know the rules. These games may have been like the African game Mancala. Many times we find these boards in places where men were bored, like in the doorways of guardposts, where the men (maybe slaves) had to sit all day in case somebody came. Somewhere in China, chess was invented and became very popular, eventually making its way west to India, then the Islamic Empire, and finally to Europe.

Gambling games were also very popular, and dice have been found from very old houses. Dice were sometimes made out of stone, and sometimes carved from bone or ivory. They had the same six numbers on them as today's square dice, arranged in the same way. And, because they were used for gambling, we even find some dice which had been loaded: a little piece of lead was hidden inside to make the die heavier on one side so it would land on that side more often! Playing cards were completely unknown in the ancient world, though people did play cards in the middle ages.

People also played games with knucklebones. Knucklebones are the vertebrae of medium-sized animals like sheep or goats, and the games you play with them are like jacks.

Other toys have also been found. Children played with *dolls*: some are made of wood and some of clay and bone. Some have jointed legs and arms, so they can move them, and others are all in one piece. This jointed doll is from Tarragona in Spain. You have to be careful though. Some little figures which look like dolls or dolls' dishes are really religious objects meant to be put in people's tombs when they died. Children had wooden blocks that they could stack up and knock down.

Festival Games

Physical development was much prized in the ancient world and apart from the training in the gymnasia there were also ball games that the youth participated in and in Roman times special ball courts were built. Also equestrian and boat races were popular but the great Festival Games were by far the most popular. It may be coincidence that this happened along with religious events as the large crowds attracted to a festival provided the spectators for the athletic competitions. Any city with enough prize-money could and did mount games, where champions were given substantial monetary rewards, but at the religious festivals the prize was generally a simple wreath. However the home town of a winner would often shower him with gifts as it had brought them such prestige. Olympic winners paid no tax, were fed free for life and much was to be gained from becoming a hero.

The Greek states and others were in a constant state of war over even the most minor causes, but or the Olympic festival, held every four years, a truce or 'ekecheiria', which means 'holding of hands' was announced before and during the games. Messangers were sent out as far away as France to the Baltic Sea. This armistice allowed visitors and competitors to travel safely to Olympia.

A bronze inscription describing the truce was displayed at Olympia. Wars were suspended, armies were prohibited from entering Elis or threatening the Games, and legal disputes and the carrying out of death penalties were forbidden. Elis had restarted the Games after a visit to the oracle at Delphi and the city itself, just north of Olympia acted as the Olympic village prior to the Games with, but during the Games all travelled to the sanctuary of Olympia which contained the great temple of Zeus and also a temple to his wife Hera. Here the elite were housed in a huge Guest House while most slept out in the open.

The athletes themselves were more often than not soldiers and even though we are used to thinking of the games as a time of peace, some events like the pancration and boxing could end in death. Violent as these two events were there were strict rules which forbad cheating as well as bringing hatred to the competition.

The most common myth surrounding the origin of the Olympic Games was that of Pelops, a prince from Lydia in Asia Minor who wished to marry the daughter of King Oinomaos.

To do so any suitor must compete against the King in a Chariot race and if he lost he would be beheaded. Pelops replaced a pin with wax in the chariot of the King who was then killed. Pelops married Hippodamia and founded the Olympic games to celebrate his victory. A different version says they were funeral games in the memory of Oinomaos. The Delphi Charioteer right and if you ever get the chance to see it up close you will be stunned to see the fine eyelashes on the statue - left.

Another myth comes from the Tenth Olympian Ode of the poet Pindar who tells how in his fifth labour, Herakles had to clean the stables of King Augeas of Elis. After disagreements, broken promises etc. Herakles sacked the city of Elis and instituted the Olympic Games in honour of his father, Zeus. He is said to have taught men how to wrestle and measured out the stade, or the length of the footrace.

Games in Ancient Greece

The Greeks took games of all kinds very seriously, but especially physical athletic competition. The Greeks believed that their gods particularly loved to see strong, fit, graceful human bodies, especially boys' and men's bodies. So one way to get on the good side of the gods was to exercise, to eat right, to oil your skin, to create a beautiful body that the gods would love. Because of the Greek tendency to turn everything into an agon, a competition, this also meant that there were a lot of athletic competitions in Greece. The most famous of these is the Olympic Games, but there were other games held in other places as well, like the Isthmian Games at Corinth.

Young men in most Greek cities spent a lot of their time training for these competitions, and the best of them were chosen to compete against the best young men from other cities. Then they would all meet, at the Olympic Games or the Isthmian Games or elsewhere, and compete for prizes and for the favor of the gods. Of course these games also served as good training for the army, because all these men would be soldiers as well. The events were the same kind as in the Olympics today: running, jumping, throwing a javelin, and throwing a discus. Only men could compete.

Greek boys also played games which were not part of the Olympic games, like field hockey. Greek boys usually played games without their clothes on. Greek girls played games like throwing balls, though the Greeks were much less interested in physical activity for girls.

Greeks also played less active games like dice and marbles, and knucklebones, and checkers. This is a famous vase from the Vatican museum showing Achilles and Ajax playing checkers. Even in these games, though, the competition was very important, and there was a feeling that losing at games meant that the gods didn't like you.

Gymnasia

As mentioned the gymnasia took it's name from the Greek word 'gymnos' meaning naked. This was a state run centre for training where men and boys met and practiced athletics and the youth also followed intellectual training. Three gymnasia in Athens - the

Lyceum, the Academy and the Cynosarges became great schools of philosophy. The physical training was in preparation for war. The complex consisted of an open courtyard for wrestling and the like, a running track, a grand colonnade (the stoa), which could also be used for training during inclement weather and an assortment of cloak rooms, oiling rooms, baths and lecture rooms. The practice of being totally naked was peculiar to Greece and does not appear to be followed elsewhere. Training was done to the accompaniment of rhythmical music and as a high emphasis was placed on both physical strength and aesthetics, a student could be eliminated for lacking in either strength or beauty of appearance. It is known that there existed special diets to compliment the physical needs of different sports.

Palaestra

This was a much simpler and privately owned school for wrestling and gymnastics and consisted of a sand covered courtyard surrounded by changing rooms.

Athletics

Used as training in preparation for war, athletics date back to the time of Homer. Much prized in Greece and always totally nude, but less popular in Rome although the more educated classes did practice the Greek sports for leisure and relaxation. The Etruscans also followed the Greek games but were clothed. The main forms were:-

– *Wrestling*: Individuals challenged according to age not weight. It was the most popular sport. The contestants oiled themselves and some dusted themselves for better grip. Three falls of the shoulder or knees touching the ground designated the winner. Biting and genital holds were illegal, but breaking your opponent's fingers was permitted. It is known that Aristotle, Plato and Hypocrites were capable wrestlers.

Pancration: A more violent form of wrestling where the opponent gave in at the point of strangulation or having a bone broken. Only biting and gouging an opponent's eyes, nose, or mouth with fingernails were banned. There were both men's and boys divisions of this sport which eventually became a highly admired.

Boxing: A continuos match which ended in a knock-out or a raised hand of submission. They wore soft leather around the fist and knuckles and even ear guards during training, but these could inflict great damage to the opponent. A referee was armed with a stick for disciplining any offence. In gladiatorial Rome the gloves were weighted with metal or spikes. There were no weight classes within the mens' and boys' divisions, and opponents were chosen randomly.

Running: A 200 metre rectangular track with starting lines, where the competitors traversed it once for a single foot race (stadion), turned and ran back for a double foot race (diaulos), or completed twelve circuits for the long distance. There was also a two to four-stadion (384 m. to 768 m.) race in armour. (the standard hoplite armour of helmet, shield, and greaves weighed about 50-60 lbs. In the 5th century BC there were even mechanical starting gates. The actual length of the stadion was said to be stepped out by Heracles who measured the 600 lengths of his rather large foot. Some festivals included a relay race where the runners ran through the streets and passed a lighted torch. Originally the goal of the race was the great altar of Zeus.

- *Long Jump*: A sport which is relatively unknown and which saw the contestant carrying weights (halteres). It may also have been from a standing position.
- *Discus*: Much like the modern equivalent. A lead, bronze, iron or stone circular plate thrown from an upward swing of a straight arm. they weighed around 7kilos but varied for men and boys. The longest throw won.
- *Javelin*: Also judged on distance thrown in the best of five but it had to hit the ground with it's point. They used a thong attached to fingers and the Javelin which added distance and spin.
- *Pentathlon*: Contestants entered five events - long jump, foot race, discus throwing, javelin and wrestling.
- *Chariot Race:* There were two and four horse chariot races, with separate races for chariots drawn by foals. Another race was between carts drawn by two mules. The course was twelve laps around the stadium track or hippodrome. The Chariot race was said to have been started by King Pelops whom myth said was buried near the Temple of Zeus.
- *Riding:* The course was six laps with separate races for full-grown horses and foals. Riders rode naked and without stirrups. As the training, equipment, and feed of both the jockey and the horses was so expensive, the owner received the olive wreath of victory instead of the rider.

Games in Ancient India

In the area of recreation and sports India had evolved a number of games. One would be surprised to know today that games like, Chess, Snakes and Ladders, Playing Cards, Polo, the martial arts of Judo and Karate had originated in India and it was from here that these games were transmitted to foreign countries, where they were further developed. At times the changes made in the original nature of the Indian sport-forms were so many and so fundamental that the game lost all similarity with its original form in India.

Some Indian games were not transmitted abroad and remained confined to India. For instance we have Kabbadi, Kho-Kho, AtyaPatya, Malkhamb, Gulli-danda, etc., which are being played today exclusively in India. In this chapter we shall look into how the games like Chess and Ludo (Snakes and Ladders), the martial art of Karate, and Playing cards had existed in India for the past 2000 years and how in some cases the indigenous form of the game became totally extinct erasing the fact that- the game had ever been played in India.

Chess

A game very similar to modern Chess and Ludo was played in ancient India. In this game there used to be four participants due to which it was named Chaturanga meaning 'four bodies'. This four-bodied game was played with counters and a dice (aksha). Another name for this game was Astapada meaning 'eight steps'. This game was perhaps the progenitor of both modern day games of Chess and Ludo. There are instances in Indian history of this game being played.

One such instance is in the Mahabharata when Pandavas and Kauravas play this game. Yudhistira the eldest of the Pandavas places his bets on his kingdom, his wife Draupadi and all other material possessions. And by a malevolent trick he loses to the Kauravas everything that he had placed his bets on. Consequently to humiliate the Pandavas, Dushasana one of the evil Kaurava brothers takes hold of Draupadi whom Yudhisthira has lost to the Kauravas, and tries to disrobe her in front of the assembled court. The Pandavas though powerful are helpless as they have lost Draupadi and according to the rules of the game they have no claim on her anymore.

In distress, Draupadi invokes Lord Srikrishna to come to her rescue. And in answer to her prayers the lord appears and in a miracle sends a continuous stream of apparel to clothe Draupadi's body. The evil Dushasana tires himself out trying to tear away Draupadi's clothes but he is powerless against the divine strength of Lord Srikrishna. After hours of struggling to achieve his evil intention he falls unconscious to the floor. Draupadi's honour is saved. In deference to Lord Srikrishna's wishes, the Kauravas relinquish their claim to Draupadi. But in return the Pandavas are obliged to relinquish their kingdom for fourteen years and go into exile in forests, after which they return and regain their kingdom from the Kauravas, but not before a devastating war is fought between the two clans on the battlefield of Kurutshetra.

The Mahabharata story throws light on the fact that a game similar to Chess was played in ancient India. The Mahabharata is variously dated around 800 and 1100 B.C. Thus this game was known in India nearly 3000 years ago. It is the view of some historians that this game was also used in the allocation of land among different members of a clan when a new settlement was being established.

The Indian origin of the game of chess is supported even by the Encylopedia Britannica according to which, "About 1783-89 Sir. William Jones, in an essay published in the 2nd Vol. of Asiatic Researches, argued that Hindustan was the cradle of chess, the game having been known there from time immemorial by the name Chaturanga, that is, the four angas, or members of an army, which are said in the Amarakosha to be elephants, horses, chariots and foot soldiers.

As applicable to real armies, the term Chaturanga is frequently used by the epic poets of India. Sir William Jones' essay is substantially a translation of the Bhawishya Purana, in which is given a description of a four-handed game of chess played with dice." "Sir William, however, grounds his opinions as to the Hindu origin of chess upon the testimony of the Persians and not upon the above manuscript," He lays it down that chess, under the Sanskrit name Chaturanga was exported from India into Persia in the 6th century of our era; that by a natural corruption, the old Persians changed the name into chatrang; but when their country was soon afterwards taken possession of by the Arabs, who had neither the initial nor the final letter of the word in their alphabet, they altered it further into Shatranj, which name found its way presently into modern Persian and ultimately into the dialects of India."

The Encyclopedia Britannica further says that Wander Linde, in his exhaustive work, Geschichte and Litteraturdes Schachspiels, has much to say of the origin-theories, nearly all of which he treats as so many myths. He agrees with those who consider that the Persians received the game from the Hindus. The outcome of his studies appears to be that chess certainly existed in Hindustan in the 8th century, and that probably that country is the land of its birth. He inclines to the idea that the game originated among the Buddhists, whose religion was prevalent in India from the 3rd to the 9th century. According to their ideas, war and slaying of one's own fellow-men, for any purpose whatever, is criminal, and the punishment of the warrior in the next world will be much worse than that of the simple murderer, hence chess was invented as a substitute for war.

According to the Encylopedia "Altogether, therefore, we find the best authorities agreeing that chess existed in

India before it is known to have been played anywhere else. In this supposition they are strengthened by the names of the game and some of its pieces. Shatranj as Forbes has pointed out, is a foreign word among the Persians and the Arabians, whereas its natural derivation from the term Chaturanga is obvious.

Again affix the Arabic name for the bishop, means the elephant, derived from alephhind, the Indian elephant." Even the word checkmate is derived from the Persian term Shah Mat which means 'the king is dead!'. The Sanskrit translation of this term would be Kshatra Mruta. Another term viz. 'the rooks' which is the name for one set of the counters used in chess, originated from the Persian term Roth which means a soldier.The Persian term according to the Encyclopedia is derived from the Indian term Rukh, which obviously seems to have originated in the Sanskrit word Rakshak which means a soldier from Raksha which means 'to protect'.

About the introduction of this game into Persia, the Encylopedia says that "The Persian poet Firdousi, in his historical poem, the Shahnama, gives an account of the introduction of Shatranj into Persia in the reign of Chosroes I Anushirwan, to whom came ambassadors from the sovereign of Hind, with a chess-board and men asking him to solve the secrets of the game, if he could or pay tribute. The king asked for seven days grace, during which time the wise men vainly tried to discover the secret. Finally, the king's minister took the pieces home and discovered the secret in a day and a night."

The Encyclopedia Britannica concludes that "Other Persian and Arabian writers state that Shatranj came into Persia from India and there appears to be a concensus of opinion that may be considered to settle the question. Thus we have the game passing from the Hindus to the Persians and then to the Arabians, after the capture V of

Persia by the Caliphs in the 7th century, and from them, directly or indirectly, to various parts of Europe, at a time which cannot be definitely fixed, but either in or before the 10th century. That the source of the European game is Arabic is clear enough, nor merely from the words "check" and "mate", which are evidently from Shah mat, but also from the names of some of the pieces".

Thus it was from India that the ancient Persians are said to have learnt this game, and from them it was transmitted to the Greco Roman world. The evidence of the Persians having borrowed this game from India is seen in the name the Persians gave to it. The Persian word for chess is Chatrang, which was later changed by the Arabs to Shatranj. As said in Encyclopedia Britannica, thig word is obviously a corruption of the Sanskrit original Chaturanga.

Karate and Judo

Many eyebrows would be raised when an Indian lays claim to the martial arts of Judo and Karate. Such askance is understandable. Everybody the world over knowns that it was the countries of the far-east China, Korea and Japan who have given these arts to us. The finest exponents of Karate, Judo come from these countries, schools like Shaolin and Ninja that have nurtured these arts are from the far-east. But in the distant corner of India a dying martial art exists which comes significantly close to Karate. This art from is called Kalaripayate. The practitioners of Kalaripayate have to develop acrobatic capabilities and use swords or knives to attack an opponent. Even an unarmed exponent of Kalaripayate presents an invincible adversary.

This art from seems to have travelled from India to the countries of the far-east alongwith the Buddhist religion. Buddhists monks who travelled barefoot and unarmed to spread the gospel of Buddha seem to have accepted this art with alterations suitable to the philosophy of nonviolence. Such a technique of defence would have been necessary for them as they travelled individually or in small groups in foreign lands during which they were exposed to dangers from bandits and fanatics from other religions. Buddhist monks seem to have tempered the originally violent character of this art. The violent and exterminative nature of Kalaripayate is evient from the daggers and knives that are used. Unlike Kalaripayate, Judo and Karate do not allow the use of lethal weapons.

The aim of a Karate practitioner is mainly to disarm and disable his opponent without mortally wounding him. This can be looked upon as a reflection of the Buddhist attitude towards life. Further both Judo and Karate are deeply interwoven with meditation unlike other martial arts like boxing, wrestling, fencing, etc. The concentration aspect in Judo and Karate perhaps stems from this. Both Judo and Karate are sought to be kept as arts to be used for just purposes for pro tection of the weak, etc.

The oath that every student of these disciplines has to take is evidence of this. A teacher of Judo or Karate traditionally commands deep respect of students and a lesson always starts with a bow of the students to the teacher. The teacher here is not looked upon only as a coach as in western martial arts like boxing and fencing. This relationship between a teacher and student in Judo and Karate could have its roots in the Guru-Shishya tradition of India.

Thus it is quite possible that these martial art forms originated in southern India and were transmitted to China, Korea and Japan by Buddhist monks. But it has to be conceded that they were neglected in India where like

Buddhism they atrophied and today the world considers them to be a legacy bequeated by the countries of the far-east.

The Egyptians engaged in many sports and honoured the body. There is also evidence of sports like bull-leaping, acrobatics, wrestling, and boxing, in Minoan Crete found on relief vases, wall frescoes, seals, and in figurines. The "Boxer Vase" from Hagia Triada in Crete has several bands of relief depicting wrestling, bull-leaping, and boxing. Leaping and somersaulting over bulls appears as early as 2000 BC. Boxing also appears and the figures show a clenched fist, and sometimes wear hand-coverings or ancient boxing gloves. The four major Minoan Palaces of Knossos, Phaestos, Mallia, and Zakro contained L shaped theatres that could hold up to 500 spectators, and central courts ideal for bull-leaping. The Minoans had extensive trading contact with the Egyptians and the sporting influence from Egypt may have passed to the Minoans and then to Greece. A subsequent invasion of the aggressive Dorians from the North may have added the competitive spirit to the games we know of in Greece.

Although records cannot verify games earlier than 776 B.C., the contests in Homer's Iliad indicate a much earlier competitive tradition. The ancient Greek games were held, every fourth summer, at Olympia, in honor of Zeus. They reached their height in the 5th–4th cent. B.C.; thereafter they became more and more professionalized until, in the Roman period, they provoked much censure. They were eventually discontinued by Emperor Theodosius I of Rome at the end of the 4th cent. A.D. Among the Greeks, the games were nationalistic in spirit; states were said to have been prouder of Olympic victories than of battles won. Women, foreigners, slaves, and dishonored persons were forbidden to compete. Contestants were required to train faithfully for 10 months before the games, had to remain 30 days under the eyes of officials in Elis, who had charge of the games, and had to take an oath that they had fulfilled the training requirements before participating. At first, the Olympic games were confined to running, but over time new events were added: the long run (720 B.C.), when the loincloth was abandoned and athletes began competing naked; the pentathlon (708 B.C.); boxing (688 B.C.); chariot racing (680 B.C.); the pankration (648 B.C.), involving boxing and wrestling contests for boys (632 B.C.); and the foot race with armor (580 B.C.).

Greek women, forbidden not only to participate in but also to watch the Olympic games, held games of their own, called the Heraea. Those were also held every four years but had fewer events than the Olympics. Known to have been conducted as early as the 6th cent. B.C., the Heraea games were discontinued about the time the Romans conquered Greece.

The winners of the Olympics (and of the Heraea) were crowned with chaplets of wild olive, and in their home city-states male champions were also awarded valuable gifts and privileges. The ancient Olympics were rather different from the modern Games. There were fewer events, and only free men who spoke Greek could compete, instead of athletes from any country. Also, the games were always held at Olympia instead of moving around to different sites every time.

Like our Olympics, though, winning athletes were heroes who put their home towns on the map. One young Athenian nobleman defended his political reputation by mentioning how he entered seven chariots in the Olympic chariotrace. This high number of entries made both the aristocrat and Athens look very wealthy and powerful. Like their modern counterparts, ancient athletes had a way of capturing the public's imagination.

Several ancient authors such as Pindar, Pausanias, Strabo, and Dio Chrysostom record the noteworthy exploits of some of the best-known Olympic victors of ancient times.

The Olympic Games were supposed to start in the Peloponnese, in Greece, some 3 000 years ago. Sports competitions were organised at Olympia and were named after their location, hence their name of Olympic Games. Nobody knows exactly when they began, but the first written mention of the competitions is dated to 776 BC years before the birth of Christ. It can be said to be the time when human civilization was at its infancy. Olympics derived its name from the ancient Greek city of Olympia where the game show was founded as a part of a big festival. Olympia had a temple of Zeus. And the festival was used to be held in the honor of Zeus. The earth goddess Gaea was originally worshiped at Olympia.

In the course of time, her importance reduced. And it was the sky god Zeus in whose honor priestly officials conducted quadrennial athletic contests. Sacred also were the games held at Delphi, in honor of Apollo, and at Corinth and Nemea. These four events were known as the periodos, and great athletes, such as Theagenes of Thasos, prided themselves on victories at all four sites. The athletic triumphs brought with it special prestige. Both in the form of statues of the victors and also material benefits. The festival witnessed the gathering of talents in different fields from different parts of the globe.

The great festival of Olympia earned so much of awe those days that even soldiers would lift no weapon during the festival. Its influence was so great that even the two warring states in Greece would announce a 'cease war' for the time being. All were eligible for taking part in the game show. Any independent Greek could take part in any event following a ten-month's training. And every state would vie for seeing their player clinching the title. Accordingly, Greeks would attach special attention to the physical culture of all boys since an early age. Some of the events those days included penthalon, pancresia, wrestling, discuss throwing, javelin throwing, running, chariot racing. The winner of each event was awarded a crown made of green olive bough. This apart, the winners were greeted with honors and a hero's welcome back home. Of all the events pancresian was the most challenging one. It was a play-until-dead type of game. The winner had to be highly skilled in multiple disciplines like wrestling, boxing, kicking.

On the other hand the winner of the penthalon had to be an expert in high jump, race, discuss and javelin throwing, and, the stand-up wrestling. Unlike the three categories found in modern boxing, ancient Olympics had no such category. Thus the heaviest weighted one would eventually wear the boxing crown. But Olympic was not only confined among the players, musicians, artists, poets - all would come to take part in events marked for them.

Since the Greeks were devoted to secular sports as well as to sacred games, no polis, or city-state, was considered a proper community if it lacked a gymnasium where, as the word gymnos indicates, naked male athletes trained and competed. Except at militaristic Sparta, Greek girls rarely participated in sports of any kind. Women were excluded from the Olympic Games even as spectators. Pausanias, the 2nd-century-AD traveler, wrote of races for girls at Olympia, but these events in honor of Hera were of minor importance.

Unfortunately the curtain fell on ancient Olympics game during the regime of the Roman emperor Theodosius. He had a strong dislike to all games and sports. He was driven by a credo that there should be no place for a barbarian game show like Olympics in the Christian civilization. Not only he ended the tradition of Olympic games, but ordered the destruction of the

Olympic temple and the stadium. And it was under his instruction the statue of Zeus was carried away to Constantinople. Later the statue was destroyed by a fire. Later his successor Theodosius II asked the destruction of all Greek temples including that of Zeus. Still, what was left out was wiped by flood and earthquake. Thus the ancient game came to an end.

Although the ancient Olympic games were first recorded in 776 BC, they originated at least a century before that and possibly as early as the 13th century BC. One Greek legend said that the great Herakles won a race at Olympia, a plain in the small state of Elis, and then decreed that the race should be re-enacted every four years.

Another said that Zeus himself had originated the festival after defeating Cronus for the sovereignty of heaven.The more likely story is that the Olympic festival was a local religious event until 884 BC, when Iphitus, the king of Elis, decided to turn it into a broader, pan-Hellenic festival. To accomplish that, he entered into a temporary truce with other rulers, allowing athletes and others to travel peacefully to Olympia while the festival was going on. The Greeks based their chronology on four-year periods called Olympiads, and the Olympic festival marked the beginning of each Olympiad. Evidently, the festival was reorganized in 776 BC, which was considered the start of the first Olympiad.

The festival was basically a religious gathering to celebrate the gods worshipped in common by all Hellenes, primarily Zeus. There were three other major pan-Hellenic festivals, the Pythian, the Nemean, and the Isthmian, all of which included fairs, but the festival at Olympia became pre-eminent by 572 BC, when Elis and Sparta entered into an alliance under which Elis was in charge of the event itself while Sparta enforced the sacred truce.

A single foot race was the only athletic event until the fifteenth Olympiad. The race was the length of the stadium, approximately 200 yards. As time went on, the games associated with the festival expanded and became increasingly important. A race of two stadium lengths was added in 724 and a long-distance race of 24 stadium lengths was added in 720.

Other types of sports followed quickly: Wrestling and the pentathlon in 708, boxing in 688, chariot racing in 680, and the pancratium, a combination of boxing and wrestling, in 748. At one time or another, there were 23 Olympic sports events, although they were never all held at the same festival.

A branch of wild olive was the only official prize for an Olympic winner, but there were also usually some unofficial prizes awarded by his city-state. For example, Athens allowed an Olympic champion to live free of charge in the Pyrtaneum, a special hall set aside for distinguished citizens. Other city-states exempted winners from taxes for an Olympiad, and in some cases citizens contributed to a cash award.

Athletes had to arrive in Elis a month before the games to undergo spiritual, moral, and physical training under the supervision of the judges, who then decided which of them were genuinely qualified to compete. Each competitor had to swear an oath that he was a free-born Greek who had committed no sacrilege against the gods.

At first, the games took up only one day of the festival. That was extended to two days in 680, with the addition of chariot racing, and to five days in 632. However, only three of those days were actually devoted to competition. The first day was devoted to religious sacrifices, the registration of athletes, and the taking of the Olympic oath. Prizes were awarded and thanksgiving sacrifices were offered on the fifth day. Athletes usually competed nude. They originally wore shorts but, according to one ancient writer, Pausanias, a competitor deliberately lost his shorts so that he could run more freely during the race in 720 BC, and clothing was then abolished.

Women were not allowed to watch the games, but that had nothing to do with the nudity of the male athletes. Rather, it was because Olympia was dedicated to Zeus and was therefore a sacred area for men. The chariot races, which were held outside the sacred precinct, were open to women spectators. At its peak during the 4th century BC, the Olympic festival drew crowds not only from the Pelopponesian Peninsula but from colonies as far away as Libya and Egypt. Poets and other writers recited spontaneously, sculptors worked on statues while surrounded by spectators, vendors sold food from stalls, traders from throughout the peninsula sold horses.

Traveling to Olympia took on the nature of a pilgrimage, which attracted some of the greatest names of Greece's classic period. Plato attended the festival when he was seventy. Demosthenes, Diogenes the Cynic, Pythagoras, and Themistocles all visited Olympia at one time or another. The young Thucydides was in the audience when Herodotus, the "father of history," read from his works.

Even after the glory that was Greece vanished, the Olympics lived on, but in a debased form under the Romans, who replaced the traditional games with their own gladiatorial contests, in which slaves replaced free-born Greeks as the competitors. In 394 AD, Theodosius the Great decreed an end to the Olympic Games. But they had lasted more than a thousand years, perhaps as long as 1600 years, and certainly longer than any other secular institution in history.

The Games were held at Olympia every four years. This four-year period acquired the name Olympiad, and was used as a date system : time was counted in Olympiads, rather than years.

The Panhellenic Games

The Games organised at Olympia led to the development of the Panhellenic Games, which also included :

- The Games at Delphi (Pythian Games)
- The Games at Corinth (Isthmian Games)
- The Games at Nemea (Nemean Games)

These Games were special because they brought the Greek world together at a time when Greece was not a single state, but a series of city-states (politically and economically inde pendent communities). From Greece and the colonies (in Italy, North Africa and Asia Minor), people travelled to take part in or attend these Games, inspired by the shared feeling of belonging to the same culture or religion. It should be noted that the four Panhellenic Games were never held during the same year. It is difficult to know exactly what gave rise to these Games. Mythology is mixed up with history, and events which happened at the time were often explained as the consequences of divine intervention. This was the case for the Panhellenic Games, for which there are numerous stories attempting to explain their origin.

The Athlete

A number of objects made by the Ancient Greeks have survived until today. Archaeological excavations have uncovered sculptures, vases, coins and tools. These objects give us a good idea about how people lived at the time. We can use them to find out more about the athletes and the competitions they participated in. When looking at a sculpture or a scene painted on a vase, it is easy to identify the athlete by his nakedness. Indeed, for both training and competitions, athletes were always nude.

Their bodies, shaped by exercise, were used as models by sculptors and painters who drew inspiration for their works directly from the athletes and their movements whilst practising sport. The beauty of the naked body was considered to reflect internal beauty and to illustrate the harmonious balance between body and mind. Practising sport helped to develop and attain this harmony.

When they arrived at the gymnasium or palaestra, athletes stripped completely. Without the protection of a layer of clothing, they had to take special care of their skin. To prepare for training, an athlete would cover his body with olive oil and then dust it with fine sand. The oil and sand combination helped to regulate his body temperature as well as providing protection from the sun and from the stick that the trainer would use to beat him if he didn't perform the exercises correctly ! After the events, the athlete would take his strigil, a curved instrument, and scrape the sweat, oil and sand off his skin. He then finished cleaning himself with water and a sponge. During competitions, athletes cared for their skin in the same way. The equipment that the athlete needed was extremely simple :

- an aryballos, a kind of small bottle, often earthenware, containing oil
- a strigil
- a sponge

These were held together by a ring which the athlete attached to the wall of the gymnasium or palaestra.

Cheating and Fines

Some athletes did not always respect their oath and tried to win by unauthorised means. This kind of cheating was punished and the dishonest athletes had to pay fines. With this money, statues of Zeus were erected, known as the Zanes. Each of these statues were placed along the passageway that led to the stadium, with the name of the cheat inscribed on its base. To get to the competition site, the athletes had to walk past all the statues. This reminded them of the example not to follow !

Famous Athletes

In the history of the modern Games, great champions are headline news. They are admired and respected : they are real heroes. The Games of Antiquity also had their champions. Thanks to their performances, the names of these famous athletes are still known today. The fabulous wrestler Milo of Croton, several times Olympic champion in a career spanning 26 years. Milo was a true hero and enjoyed many other victories in competitions outside Olympia. Famous for his legendary power, he was also known for his great appetite ! The extraordinary Leonidas of Rhodes, fourtime Olympic running champion, was considered the equal of a god by his fellow countrymen. There was also the boxer Melankomas of Caria (Asia Minor), who was famous not only for his magnificent body, but also for his unusual fighting technique. Melankomas did not strike his opponents but instead wore them out by skilfully dodging their blows ! After they died, the great champions had special honours bestowed upon them. So that their victories at the Games were never forgotten, their tombs were decorated with a gravestone on which images of the wreaths won during their careers were carved.

Sports on the programme

In the ancient world, the Olympic Games were a reference point. The sports on the programme in Olympia were often taken up with slight variations at other Panhellenic sites or, with further minor variations, in local competitions. It is the Olympic programme that is presented here. The programme of the Games comprised only individual sports - team sports were not included. No water sports figured on the programme either.

Arrangements for the Games

The opening of the Games was marked by animal sacrifices on the altar of Zeus. The competitions, which eventually lasted for some five days, took place in the stadium and the hippodrome. The stadium was made of hard-packed earth and was rectangular in shape. There were no terraces and the spectators sat on the banks, except for the officials who were provided with a stand. Free men, slaves and young girls were able to watch the Games. Only married women were excluded from the crowd of spectators. The Games ended with banquets organised in honour of the winner and with sacrifices in honour of Zeus.

With the exception of the equestrian sports, which were staged in the hippodrome, all the competitions were held in the stadium. There were different types of race :

- The stade or stadion, which consisted of one length of the stadium
- The diaulos, two lengths or double stadium
- The dolichos, a long-distance race (from 7 to 24 laps)
- The armed race (in Olympia it was a diaulos), where the athletes wore a helmet and greaves, and carried a shield

The competitors took their place at a starting line marked out by white limestone slabs. They ran in a straight line and not around the stadium as they do today.

Javelin Throwing

A leather strap was fixed to the shaft of the javelin to form a loop. When throwing, the athlete inserted his index and second fingers into the loop, which allowed him to increase the distance the javelin travelled.

Long Jump

The athlete used weights. With his feet together and without a run-up, the athlete jumped, throwing his arms forward. In the air, arms and legs were almost parallel. Before landing, the athlete swung his arms backwards, dropping the weights at the same time. This movement propelled his legs forward and extended the distance of the jump. The use of weights meant that the athletes' movements had to be co-ordinated. Flute music accompanied the event in order to aid the participants in this respect. The weights were made of stone or metal and their shape varied.

Combat Sports

There are several hypotheses concerning the place where wrestling, pugilism and pankration events took place. Some researchers think that these competitions took place in the Altis, in front of the altar of Zeus. Others believe they took place in the stadium. The drawing of lots decided which athletes would compete against each other. Unlike today, there were no weight categories.

Wrestling

The opponents fought standing up, with bare hands. There were different types of hold. The person who first touched the ground three times was the loser.

Pankration

A type of wrestling. All moves were allowed in pankration, except for biting, gouging out eyes and putting fingers in the opponent's nose.

Boxing

The fighters' hands were protected by long leather thongs. These ancestors of boxing gloves underwent numerous modifications over time. Pieces of metal were added on the knuckles, making the punches much more violent.

Penathlon

The pentathlon comprised five events : running, jumping, discus throwing, javelin throwing and wrestling. The athlete who took part in this competition was called a pentathlos. It was the most all-round sport, and the body of the pentathlos was considered to be the most perfect.

Equestrian Events

Chariot racing and horse riding took place in the hippodrome. Chariot races were spectacular and particularly popular with the public. There were quadriga races, where the chariots were pulled by four horses, and biga races, where the chariots were pulled by two horses. The drivers were called charioteers. Unlike the athletes, the charioteers were not naked but instead wore long tunics. In the horse races, the jockeys were naked. They rode bare-back (without a saddle) and did not wear spurs. Thanks to the equestrian events, women participated indirectly in the Games ! As owners, they could race their horses, driven or ridden by male charioteers or jockeys.

Music and Singing

Music and singing competitions were not on the programme of the Olympic Games. They were a speciality of the Games at Delphi ! Well before the appearance of sports competitions, musical competitions were organised in Delphi. These comprised singing accompanied by the cithara (a type of lyre), flute solos or singing with flute accompaniment. Music and singing remained a feature of the Pythian Games even after the integration of sports competitions. Poetry and drama competitions also figured on the programme.

Modern Olympic Games: 1896-1964

The modern revival of the Olympic games is due in a large measure to the efforts of Pierre, baron de Coubertin, of France. They were held, appropriately enough, in Athens in 1896, but that meeting and the ones that followed at Paris (1900) and at St. Louis (1904) were hampered by poor organization and the absence of worldwide representation. The first successful meet was held at London in 1908; since then the games have been held in cities throughout the world. World War I prevented the Olympic meeting of 1916, and World War II the 1940 and 1944 meetings. The number of entrants, competing nations, and events have increased steadily. To the traditional events of track and field athletics, which include the decathlon and heptathlon, have been added a host of games and sports—archery, badminton, baseball and softball, basketball, boxing, canoeing and kayaking, cycling, diving, equestrian contests, fencing, field hockey, gymnastics, judo and taekwondo, the modern pentathlon, rowing, sailing, shooting, soccer, swimming, table tennis, team (field) handball, tennis, trampoline, the triathlon, volleyball, water polo, weight lifting, and wrestling. Olympic events for women made their first appearance in 1912.

A separate series of winter Olympic meets, inaugurated (1924) at Chamonix, France, now includes ice hockey, curling, bobsledding, luge, skeleton, and skiing, snowboarding, and skating events. Since 1994 the winter games have been held in even-numbered years in which the summer games are not contested. Until late in the 20th cent. the modern Olympics were open only to amateurs, but the governing bodies of several sports now permit professionals to compete as well. As a visible focus of world energies, the Olympics have been prey to many factors that thwarted their ideals of world cooperation and athletic excellence. As in ancient Greece, nationalistic fervor has fostered intense rivalries that at times threatened the survival of the games. Although officially only individuals win Olympic medals, nations routinely assign political significance to the feats of their citizens and teams. Between 1952 and 1988 rivalry between the United States and the Soviet Union, rooted in mutual political antagonism, resulted in each boycotting games hosted by the other.

Politics has influenced the Olympic games in other ways, from the propaganda of the Nazis in Berlin to pressures leading to the exclusion of white-ruled Rhodesia from the Munich games. At Munich, nine Israeli athletes were kidnapped and murdered by Palestinian terrorists. The International Olympic Committee (IOC), which sets and enforces Olympic policy, has struggled with the licensing and commercialization of the games, the need to schedule events to accommodate American television networks, and the monitoring of athletes who seek illegal competitive advantages, often through the use of performance-enhancing drugs. The IOC itself has also been the subject of controversy. In 1998 a scandal erupted with revelations that bribery and favoritism had played a role in the awarding of the 2002 Winter Games to Salt Lake City, Utah, and in the selection of some earlier venues. As a result, the IOC instituted a number of reforms including, in 1999, initiating age and term limits for members and barring them from visiting cities bidding to be Olympic sites.

Today, the Olympic Games are the world's largest pageant of athletic skill and competitive spirit. They are also displays of nationalism, commerce and politics. These two opposing elements of the Olympics are not a modern invention. The conflict between the Olympic movement's high ideals and the commercialism or political acts which accompany the Games has been noted since ancient times.

Modern Olympic Games: 1968-2004

The 1968 Olympics: Mexico City, Mexico

Fast Facts

Host City:	Mexico City, Mexico
Opening date:	Oct. 12, 1968
Closing date:	Oct. 27, 1968
Nations:	112
Athletes:	5,530 athletes (780 women, 4,750 men)
Events:	172 events in 20 sports

The over polite fiction is that the Olympics are somehow above politics. Of course, they never have been, but in 1968 politics became a much more noticeable aspect of the Olympic scene than ever before. The choice of Mexico City had been controversial anyway. The high altitude, more than 7500 feet above sea level, meaning a 30-percent reduction in available oxygen, was the problem that most critics fastened on. But there was also the fact that the Olympics had never before been awarded to an underdeveloped country, and there were doubts as to whether Mexico could possibly be ready in time.

The International Olympic Committee added its own untimely controversy by deciding to readmit segregated South Africa to competition, on the grounds that the country planned to enter an integrated team. About 40 countries announced that they would boycott the games if South Africa were admitted. In the United States, sociologist Harry Edwards was already trying to persuade black athletes to boycott the Olympics, and his movement, the Olympic Project for Human Rights, gained even more momentum.

The IOC eventually decided to continue its ban of South Africa, and the boycotts didn't take place. Nevertheless, the Black Power movement was to manifest itself in Mexico City. About two months before the Olympics, Warsaw Pact troops moved into Czechoslovakia to put down an anti-Soviet uprising. Czech gymnast Vera Caslavska, who had signed a resolution advocating democratic change, had to go into hiding in a small town where she couldn't train. She, too, was make a reappearance at the Olympics.

Ten days before the opening ceremonies, students demonstrated in Mexico City as part of a movement that had begun several months earlier. Troops fired into the crowd, killing about 250 unarmed demonstrators.

Despite all the doubts and turmoil, the Olympics went on as planned. The high altitude did take its toll on distance runners, but it also contributed to some remarkable records in shorter events. Bob Beamon's long jump of 29 feet 2 1/2 inches, the first jump ever to exceed 28 feet, was the most dramatic example, but there were others. Lee Evans' time of 43.86 in the 400-meter run stood for nearly 20 years; the United States 4x100-meter relay team set a record of 2:56.16 that lasted 24 years; and two triple jumpers exceeded the former world record without even winning medals, because three other competitors broke the record by even greater margins.

There were many other highlights. Al Oerter won his fourth gold medal in the discus. Dick Fosbury started a revolution in the high jump by winning the event with his unorthodox "Fosbury Flop," clearing the bar head first and backwards. Wyomia Tyus became the first runner of either sex to repeat as the 100-meter champion, and Debbie Myer became the first swimmer to win three individual gold medals at a single Olympics.

The biggest winner, though, was Vera Caslavska. After three weeks in hiding, she was given permission to compete in Mexico City. She responded by winning six medals, four gold and two silver. A day after the gymnastics competition ended, Caslavska was married to Josef Odlozil, a runner on the Czech track team.

Tommie Smith turned in perhaps the most courageous victory of the Olympics. He suffered a severe groin pull in the semi-finals of the 200-meter and thought he would probably be unable to run in the final. But he made it to the starting line, his thighs heavily wrapped in tape. Somehow, he fought through the pain and not only won the gold medal but set a new record of 19.83 seconds.

Smith's teammate at San Jose State, John Carlos, finished third. They were both members of the Olympic Project for Human Rights and they had agreed to stage some kind of protest if they won medals. When Smith and Carlos mounted the dais for the victory ceremony, they wore black socks and no shoes. Each wore one black glove, Smith on his right hand, Carlos on his left hand. When the National Anthem began, they lowered their heads, refusing to look at the flag, and each raised his gloved fist in the Black Power salute.

The IOC ordered the U. S. Olympic Committee to ban Smith and Carlos from further competition and to throw them out of the Olympic Village. To its credit, the

USOC initially refused. Then the IOC threatened to ban the entire U. S. track and field team from competition, forcing the USOC to give in. Incidentally, this was the same IOC that had declined to comment when Mexican troops shot down students, calling it "an internal affair."

The 1972 Olympics: Munich, Germany

Fast Facts

Host City: Munich, Germany

Opening date: Aug. 26, 1972

Closing date: Sept. 11, 1972

Nations: 121

Athletes: 7,123 athletes (1,058 women, 6,065 men)

Events: 195 events in 23 sports

The 1972 Olympics were supposed to celebrate peace. But, on Sept. 5, the 11th day of the games, Palestinian terrorists destroyed the illusion of peace by raiding the Olympic Village, killing two Israelis and taking nine others hostage. The tragedy culminated in a battle at a military airport, where the other hostages were killed, along with five of the terrorists and a German policemen. The Olympics were put on hold while a memorial service was held in the main stadium. After a 34-hour hiatus, they resumed.

Bracketing the bloodshed, the Munich games delivered more than the usual Olympic share of athletic excitement and disappointment. U. S. swimmer Mark Spitz won a record-setting seven gold medals, giving him nine for his career. Tiny Soviet gymnast Olga Korbut was the television star of the games, winning the nickname "the Munchkin of Munich" as she won two gold medals and a silver.

Liselott Linsenhoff of West Germany became the first woman to win an individual gold medal in an equestrian event when she captured the dressage championship. Finland's Lasse Viren fell while running fifth halfway through the 10,000-meter final. But he picked himself up, quickly moved into second place, and not only won the gold but set a world record by running an incredible 56.4-second final lap. Viren went on to win three more gold medals in subsequent Olympics.

In basketball, the United States' 62-game winning streak came to a controversial end in the gold medal game against the Soviet Union. With three seconds left on the clock, the U. S. led, 50-49. Two seconds after the Soviet team inbounded the ball, the head referee suddenly called an official timeout for a consultation at the scorers' table. The Soviet coach insisted that he had called a timeout while Doug Collins was making the free throw that gave the U. S. its lead.

The timeout was awarded with one second left, and the U. S. team celebrated when time ran out after the Soviets inbounded the ball without getting a shot off.

But the secretary-general of the international federation, R. William Jones of Great Britain, ordered that three seconds be put back on the clock and the Soviet team was given another chance. This time, Aleksandr "Sasha" Belov caught the long inbounds pass and scored after pushing through two U. S. defenders, giving the USSR a victory. A protest was rejected on a 3-2 vote by a jury of appeal and the U. S. team voted not to accept its silver medals. They are still stored in a Swiss bank vault.

There was further disappointment for the United States in track, as Valery Borzov of the Soviet Union won gold medals in both the 100- and 200-meter dashes. The top two U. S. sprinters failed to reach the 100-meter final because they missed their quarter-final heats due to a coach's error in reading the schedule. However, Borzov won the 200-meter so convincingly that it's doubtful an American runner could have beaten him in the shorter sprint, anyway.

For the record, the Munich Olympics were the biggest ever, up to that time. A record 121 nations and 7,123 athletes competed in a 195 events, also a record. Two former Olympic sports were restored to the program, archery after 52 years and team handball after 36 years. Slalom (whitewater) canoeing was also added.

The 1976 Olympics: Montreal, Canada

Fast Facts

Host City:	Montreal, Canada
Opening date:	July 17, 1976
Closing date:	Aug. 1, 1976
Nations:	92
Athletes:	6,028 athletes (1,247 women, 4,781 men)
Events:	198 events in 21 sports

The Montreal Games ran into serious problems before they even began. The original budget of $310 million (American) grew to nearly $1 billion because of bad management, poor planning, and just plain corruption, plunging the city of Montreal, the province of Quebec, and the nation of Canada into heavy debt to pay the tab.

Meanwhile, Tanzania exhorted African nations to boycott the Olympics if New Zealand was allowed to compete. The rationale was that New Zealand's national rugby team had toured South Africa, which was still following its apartheid policy. Even though rugby isn't an Olympic sport, 23 nations took part in the boycott.

A few weeks before the games were to begin, Canadian Prime Minister Pierre Trudeau announced that athletes from Taiwan wouldn't be allowed to compete under the name of the Republic of China. Trudeau held firm against protests from the International Olympic Committee, and Taiwanese athletes stayed home. Once the opening ceremony began,though, everything went smoothly. It was a very quiet Olympics for the United States, which won only 84 medals, finishing third behind the Soviet Union and East Germany. The men's swimming team was dominant, winning 12 of 13 events and capturing both gold and silver in 11 of the individual events. John Naber was the top performer, winning four gold medals.

As in 1972, the media star was a young female gymnast, 14-year-old Nadia Comaneci of Romania, who supplanted Olga Korbut. Comaneci was actually a much better gymnast than Korbut. She became a focus of attention when her performance on the uneven bars during the team competition won her the first perfect score of 10.0 in Olympic history. She went on to win six more perfect scores, along with five individual medals, including three golds.

The biggest track and field star was Alberto Juantorena of Cuba, the first runner to score a double in the 400- and 800-meter runs. Two athletes won gold in their events for the third straight time: Klaus Dibiasi of Italy in platform diving and Viktor Saneyev of the Soviet Union in the triple jump.

East Germany's strong showing, led by its women's swimming team, was the surprise of the 1976 Olympics. In 1972, East German women didn't win a single gold medal in swimming. In 1976, they won 11 of the 13 events. Many suspected that this sudden emergence owed at least as much to steroids as to skill and training. Sadly, they were to be proven right more than 20 years later, after Germany was reunified and former East

German coaches and doctors went on trial for giving steroids to young athletes, usually without their knowledge. No new sports were added to the 1976 Olympic program, but women competed in basketball, rowing, and team handball for the first time.

The 1980 Olympics: Moscow, Russia

Fast Facts

Host City: Moscow, Russia

Opening date: July 19, 1980

Closing date: Aug. 3, 1980

Nations: 80

Athletes: 5,217 athletes (1,124 women, 4,093 men)

203 events in 21 sports

In 1980, the Olympics were held in a Communist bloc country for the first time. They also faced the first genuinely major boycott in Olympic history. After the Soviet Union invaded Afghanistan in December of 1979, President Jimmy Carter threatened to boycott the Games if the invasion continued. The Soviets didn't back down. Led by the United States, 65 nations refused to send teams to Moscow.

The governments of Great Britain and Italy supported the boycott but allowed their athletes to compete if they wanted to. Two of those who did were British middle distance runners Steve Ovett and Sebastian Coe. Though they were countrymen, they hadn't raced against one another since 1978. Coe had set new world records in the 800-meter, 1500-meter, and 1-mile runs in 1979, but Ovett broke Coe's 1-mile record and tied his 1500-meter mark less than a month before the Olympics.

The 800-meter final was anti-climactic, as Ovett won easily but in a very slow time, nearly three seconds slower than Coe's world record, though he finished well ahead of Coe. The 1500-meter was an exciting, three-man race. Jurgen Straub of East Germany held the lead with 200 meters to go, but Coe and Ovett then turned on their finishing sprints. Straub held off Ovett, but Coe passed him to win by 4 meters, thanks to a remarkable 52.2 seconds in the final lap.

Despite the fact that only 80 nations competed, the lowest number since 1956, the Moscow Olympics produced 74 Olympic records and 36 world records, more than had been set in Montreal four years earlier. Cuba's Teófilo Stevenson breezed through the super-heavyweight division with ease, becoming the first boxer to win three gold medals in the same weight class.

The swimming field was seriously depleted by the absence of U. S. competitors, but Vladimir Salnikov of the Soviet Union not only won gold in the 1500-meter freestyle, he became the first to break the 15-minute mark in the event. Salnikov also won two other gold medals.

Another Soviet, gymnast Aleksandr Dityatin, became the first athlete to win eight medals at a single Olympics.

The 1984 Olympics: Los Angeles, California

Fast Facts

Host City: Los Angeles, California

Opening date: July 28, 1984

Closing date: Aug. 12, 1984

Nations: 140

Athletes: 6,797 athletes (1 567 women, 5,230 men)

Events: 221 events in 23 sports

In 1932, Los Angeles created the Olympic Village. In 1984, the city's organizing committee, led by Peter Ueberroth, created an entirely new model for the games.

The 1984 Olympics were the first since 1896 to be organized without major government financing. Ueberroth led a much-criticized drive for private money that even included sponsorship of the Olympic torch run, at $3,000 a kilometer.

The drive was so successful that the Games actually turned a profit of well over $200 million. The Soviet Union boycotted the Olympics, in retribution for the U. S.-led boycott of its 1980 Games, and was joined by 13 other nations. Nevertheless, a record 140 nations competed at Los Angeles, compared to only 80 at Moscow, and the number of athletes reached nearly 7,000, very close to the previous record.

The women's program continued to expand with the addition of the marathon in track and the road race in cycling, along with two sports for women only, rhythmic gymnastics and synchronized swimming.

Although the Soviet-led boycott had much less impact on the total numbers than the boycott of 1980, or even the African boycott of 1976, it had a major impact on competition. The 14 Soviet bloc countries that stayed away had won more than half the gold medals in 1976.

The sports most affected were gymnastics, weightlifting, freestyle wrestling, and women's track. The U. S. team was the chief beneficiary, increasing its medal total to 174, nearly double its total of 94 medals in 1976.

The presence of the boycotting countries wouldn't have had any effect on Carl Lewis's record-tying performance, though. Before the Olympics, Lewis had vowed to match Jesse Owens' 1936 feat of winning gold medals in both sprints, the long jump, and the 4x100-meter relay. He did it with relative ease. Lewis won the 100-meter dash by 8 feet, the largest margin in Olympic history. His 200-meter victory margin was an ample 4 feet, his gold medal long jump was nearly a foot better than anyone else's, and he anchored the relay team to a world record 37.83 seconds, nearly 8/10 of a second better than second-place Jamaica.

Women's gymnastics produced its first U. S. heroine, 16-year-old Mary Lou Retton, who scored two perfect 10s while winning the all-around championship. She also won a silver and two bronze medals. Sebastian Coe of Great Britain became the first man to repeat as 1500-meter medalist and Pertti Karpinnen of Finland won the single sculls event for the third straight time.

The 1988 Olympics: Seoul, South Korea

Fast Facts

Host City: Seoul, South Korea

Opening date: Sept. 17, 1988

Closing date: Oct. 2, 1988

Nations: 149

Athletes: 8,465 athletes (2,186 women, 6,279 men)

Events: 237 events in 24 sports

The 1988 Olympics faced a small boycott, led by North Korea and joined by Cuba, Ethiopia, and Nicaragua. Nevertheless, a record 159 nations and 8,465 athletes competed in Seoul.

Table tennis was added to the Olympic program and tennis was restored after a 62-year absence. Another new event was the women's match sprint in cycling, which led to a record that will never be broken. East German Christa Luding-Rothenburger, who won the silver medal in the match sprint, had won gold and silver speed skating medals at the Winter Olympics in February. She's the only athlete to medal at both Olympics in the same year. Since the Summer and Winter games are now held in different years, no one will ever do it again.

The top winners in Seoul were both swimmers. Kristin Otto of East Germany won six gold medals and Matt Biondi of the U. S. won a total of seven medals, including two gold. In track, sisters-in-law Florence Griffith "Flo-Jo" Joyner and Jackie Joyner-Kersee won a total of six medals. Flo-Jo won four of them, including three golds, and Joyner-Kersee won gold medals in the long jump and the heptathlon.

The biggest story to emerge from the 1988 Olympics was the disqualification of Canadian sprinter Ben Johnson after he had apparently set a world record of 9.79 seconds in the 100-meter dash. Johnson tested positive for steroids, so his world record and gold medal were both disallowed. The medal went to second-place finisher Carl Lewis, who thus became the first athlete to win that event twice. Lewis also won the long jump in more straightforward fashion, and he was the first to win two golds in that event, as well.

U. S. Diver Greg Louganis turned in the Games' most courageous performance in the springboard competition. During his ninth dive of the preliminaries, Louganis hit his head on the board, suffering a gash that required four temporary stitches.

He returned 35 minutes later, just in time to perform his last dive and advance into the finals. He went on to win gold in the springboard and, a week later, in platform diving, becoming the first male diver to win both events at two Olympics.

The 1992 Olympics: Barcelona, Spain

Fast Facts

Host City: Barcelona, Spain
Opening date: July 25, 1992
Closing date: Aug. 9, 1992

Nations: 169
Athletes: 9,367 athletes (2,708 women, 6,659 men)
Events: 257 events in 28 sports

Spain's pitch for the 1992 Olympics emphasized the 500th anniversary of Christopher Columbus's discovery of America under the auspices of the Spanish monarchy. Columbus and the explorers who followed him obviously changed the world. But the world had also changed dramatically since the 1988 Olympics. South Africa had finally abandoned apartheid and was welcomed back to the Olympics for the first time since 1960. Every nation with a National Olympic Committee was represented at Barcelona. And there were more of them than ever before because of the breakup of the Soviet Union into 15 different countries. Lithuania had an independent team for the first time since 1928, and Estonia and Latvia returned to the Olympics after being absent since 1936. Other former Soviet republics competed as the "Unified Team." There was one less country in the world, though, because of the fall of the Berlin Wall and the reunification of Germany.

Badminton, baseball, and women's judo were added to the program in 1992. And basketball was opened to professionals for the first time, allowing the U. S. "Dream Team" to stock up on NBA players, led by Larry Bird, Magic Johnson, and Michael Jordan.

The biggest individual star was Belarus gymnast Vitaly Scherbo, who won six gold medals. Derartu Tulu of Ethiopia won the women's 10,000-meter run to become the first black African woman gold medalist ever. Andreas Keller of Germany extended a family tradition as a member of Germany's gold medal field hockey team. His father had played for the 1972 gold medal team, his grandfather for the 1936 silver medal team. The most exciting contest of the games was the women's 100-meter dash. Gail Devers of the United States won in 10.82 seconds, just 1/100 second ahead of Juliet Cuthbert of Jamaica and only 6/100 faster than Merlene Ottey, also of Jamaica, who finished fifth. The major surprise was Voula Patoulidou's victory in the women's 100-meter hurdles. Patoulidou, who had never before won a major championship, was the first Greek woman ever to win a medal and the first Greek athlete to win a track and field gold medal since 1912.

The 1996 Olympics: Atlanta, Georgia

Fast Facts

Host City: Atlanta, Georgia

Opening date: July 19, 1996

Closing date: Aug. 4, 1996

Nations: 197

Athletes: 10,320 athletes (3,523 women, 6,797 men)

Events: 271 events in 26 sports

The Atlanta Olympics of 1996 were widely regarded as an athletic success but an artistic failure. A host of problems with logistics and organization plagued the games. The much-touted computerized scoring and results system kept crashing and the transportation system was inadequate. Atlanta never got around to building an Olympic village; instead, athletes were housed in dorms at Georgia Tech University.

On July 27, eight days after the opening ceremony, a bomb exploded in Centennial Olympic Park, killing one person and injuring more than 100 others. Although the park seemed to be part of the Olympic setting, it wasn't, and therefore it was not covered by Olympic security.

Atlanta set new records across the board: 197 nations send 10,320 athletes, 79 nations won medals, and 53 won gold medals. Beach volleyball, lightweight rowing, mountain biking, soccer, and women's softball were added to the program, bringing the number of events to a record 271.

Four was the lucky number for U. S. track star Carl Lewis. By taking the gold medal in the high jump, he became one of only three athletes to win the same event four times, and he also became the fourth athlete to win nine gold medals during his career.

But Lewis was overshadowed by teammate Michael Johnson, who set a world record of 19.32 seconds in the 200-meter dash and became the first male runner to double in the 200 and 400-meter events. Marie-Jose Perec of France scored the same double on the women's side.

Three athletes won their third gold medals in a single event: Krisztina Egerszegi of Hungary in the 200-meter backstroke, Aleksandr Karelin of Russia in Greco-Roman wrestling, and Naim Suleymanoglu of Turkey in weightlifting. They were surpassed by Birgit Schmidt of Germany, who won a fifth gold medal in kayaking. She had won her first in 1980.

The 2000 Olympics: Sydney, Australia

Fast Facts

Host City: Sydney, Australia

Opening date: Sept. 15, 2000

Closing date: Oct. 1, 2000

Nations: 199

Athletes: 10,651 athletes (4,069 women, 6,582 men)

Events: 300 events in 30 sports

When Juan Antonio Samaranch said that the 2000 Olympics were the best ever, it could have been taken as hyperbole. But the IOC president was simply echoing what had been said by thousands of spectators who had come to Sydney, Australia, from around the world, including many journalists who had covered several previous Olympics.

In terms of numbers, the Sydney Games surpassed all that had come before. Records were set for events (300), sports (28), countries participating (199), athletes (10,651), and the number of countries winning medals (80). The quality of the 2000 Olympics went far beyond numbers, though. Bud Greenspan, producer of the official documentary on the games, said that the torch relay and the opening ceremony both earned perfect 10s and that the rest of the organization lived up to that standard. And Greenspan had attended every Olympics since 1952.

More than 50,000 unpaid volunteers worked to make the Games successful, and foreign visitors saluted them, almost unanimously, for their friendliness as well as their efficiency. Boston Globe columnist Dan Shaughnessy wrote, "Sydney's greatest tourist attraction is its population."

The only real black spot was that more than 30 athletes failed drug tests. Even that was seen by many as a positive indication that testing was catching up to methods of hiding drug use. But on to the athletes, who produced some remarkable accomplishments. British rower Steve Redgrave became the first athlete to win gold medals at five consecutive Olympics.

Birgit Fischer of Germany won two gold medals in canoeing, giving her a total of nine medals overall, six gold, and becoming the first woman to win medals 20 years apart.

Cuban heavyweight boxer Felix Savon, Czech javelin thrower Jan Zelezny, and Greek weightlifter Pyrros Dimas all won their third consecutive gold medals. But Turkey's Naim Suleymanoglu, trying for his fourth consecutive gold in weightlifting, was eliminated from medal contention in the 62-kilogram class.

The Australian three-day event team also won a third straight gold medal, the first time that had ever been accomplished in equestrian competition. There were two major upsets. Domenico Fioravanti of Italy, ranked 14th in the world, won the 100-meter breaststroke. And Greco-Roman wrestler Rulon Gardner of the U. S. went from obscurity to world fame by beating Russia's Alexander Kareline for the super heavyweight gold medal. Kareline had won three gold medals and nine consecutive world championships, going 12 years without a single loss.

The most successful of all American athletes in 2000 was considered a failure by some. Sprinter/long jumper Marion Jones went to Sydney hoping to win five gold medals, and sometimes outright predicting it. She won five medals, but "only" three were gold, the other two bronze. The fact that she was the first athlete of either sex to win five medals in track and field at a single Olympics was often overlooked. Perhaps the most unusual gold medal victory went to the U. S. softball team. The women entered the Olympics as heavy favorites, having won 112 games in a row. But they lost three straight in the Olympic tournament, then came back to take the gold by winning three games in two days.

THE 2004 OLYMPICS: ATHENS, GREECE

Fast Facts

Host City: Athens, Greece

Opening date: Aug. 13, 2004

Closing date: Aug. 29, 2004
Nations: 201
Athletes: 11,099
Events: 301 events in 28 sports

Athens remained the host, though, and everything was ready in time. Well, almost everything. There was no roof on the natatorium, so swimmers struggled with hot sun and high temperatures during afternoon preliminaries. Medal races were fortunately held at night, when the air and water were cooler.

There was praise for the architecture of new and refurbished Olympic venues, for the fountains and reflecting pools that ornamented the areas, for the shimmering Wall of Nations created by Spanish architect Santiago Calatrava, who also designed the new stadium and the Olympic Sport Center. Besides building the obligatory new structures, Athens could serve up tradition as no other host city ever could. The men's and women's shot put competition took place in the stadium of Ancient Olympia.

The Panathinaiko Stadium, where the first modern Olympic Games were held in 1896, was modified to host archery competition and the finish of the marathon. The Karaiskaki Stadium, which had been the velodrome in 1896, was totally renovated to host men's and women's soccer. And the marathon followed the historic route from Marathon to Athens, first run by a military courier named Phidippides in 490 B.C., according to legend.

Then, suddenly, the spectators began to show up. The 70,000-seat stadium was virtually sold out for every night of the track and field competition, and other venues were nearly filled during the final week or so of the Olympics. At the closing ceremony on Aug. 29, IOC President Jacques Rogge proclaimed to the Greek people,

"You have won. You have won by brilliantly meeting the tough challenge of holding the games. These were unforgettable, dream games."

In truth, there were some problems, but for the most part they couldn't be blamed on the Athens organizing committee. The biggest controvery arose in gymnastics, where three judges were suspended for a scoring error that gave American Paul Hamm the all-around gold medal that should have gone to Yang Tae-young of South Korea. The International Gymnastics Federation said it couldn't change the result because there was no timely protest. South Korea has filed an appeal with the Court of Arbitation for Sport (CAS).

The CAS had intervened earlier in a controversy over the three-day equstrian event. Judges originally ruled that Bettina Hoy of Germany had made an illegal start, but then changed their decision and awarded Hoy the gold medal. Her score also gave Germany the gold medal in the team event. However, the CAS ruled that the original decision was correct. As a result, Hoy and Germany both dropped into fourth place. Leslie Law of Great Britain was declared the individual winner and France became the winner of the team event.

The only security breach was a bizarre incident that marred the men's marathon, the final competition before the closing ceremony. A defrocked Irish priest with a history of such disturbances burst from the crowd and grabbed Vanderlei de Lima of Brazil, who was leading the race with about three miles to go. De Lima managed to break free, but he kept looking warily over his shoulder for the rest of the race. He finished third and a protest from Brazil's track federation, asking that he be given a share of the gold medal, was rejected. That case, too, may be going to the CAS.

The individual star of the Olympics was unquestionably U. S. swimmer Michael Phelps, who won six gold medals and two bronze. The 19-year-old Phelps can become the all-time leading medal winner in Olympic history by winning four more in 2008.

Another U. S. swimmer, Natalie Coughlin, was the leading medal winner among women athletes. She won five, including two golds. Kayaker Birgit Fischer of Germany quietly moved up the all-time list of medal winners. She won a gold and silver, giving her 12 medals overall, including eight golds. Fischer won her first gold medal in 1980, when she was 18, making her the youngest women ever to win an Olympic kayaking event. With her victory as a member of the four-woman kayaking team, she became the first woman to win Olympic medals 24 years apart.

The U. S. Olympic Committee had set a goal of 100 medals and the team exceeded that by three. One of those 103 medals was a bronze for the men's basketball team. The fourth edition of the "Dream Team" was a hastily-assembled melange of players who showed little chemistry or cohesion in losing three games.

Unfortunately, that performance drew much more media attention than the U. S. women's gold medal in basketball. And the U. S. women's soccer team also won gold in an overtime match against Brazil, while the men's team didn't even qualify for the Olympic tournament. China, which will host the 2008 Olympics, was third to the U. S. and Russia in total medal standings, but was a close second in gold medals, with 32 to 35 for the United States.

4

Asian Games

Unofficial historical data traces the origination of the Asian Games to the Eastern Olympics inaugurated in Manila, the Philippines, in 1913 with 6 member countries of the Philippines, Thailand, China, Japan, Malaysia, and Hong Kong. This bienniel sports meet changed name to the Far East Championship, and continued to be held till 1934, and two years later as the Eastern Championship held in Tokyo in 1934.

From 1913 to 1934, 10 Far East Championships were held in Asia, but the championships stopped because of the outbreak of World War II. After the war a number of Asian countries became independent, their economy and culture developed, and Asian people had an increasing desire to become less isolated from each other and strengthen mutual intercourse. In order to keep abreast of the times, the Indian Prime Minister, Jawahalal Nehru, proposed an Asian sports meet in 1947 at a conference on relations between Asian countries.

In August 1948, during the 14th Olympic Games held in London, India proposed to sports leaders of the Asian teams the idea of having discussions about holding the Asian Games. As a brainchild of Professor Guru Dutt Sondhi, with assistance from Korea, Taiwan, India, the Philippines, Burma and Ceylon, the concept of the Asian Games was formalized at New Delhi in 1949.

A preparatory committee was set up to draft the charter for the Asian Amateur Athletic Federation. In February, 1949, the Asian Amateur Athletic Federation was formally formed, and its name was changed to the Asian Athletic Federation. It was decided to hold the first Asian Games in 1950 in New Dehli, the capital of India. Since then the Asian Games has been regularly held once every four years.

At the General Meeting of the Asian Games Federation in 1982, the participants agreed to the formation of the Olympic Council of Asia. This body has since then been the official governing body of the Asian Games.

The following is a quick listing of the host cities of the previous Games:

1st Asian Games	1951	New Delhi (India)
2nd Asian Games	1954	Manila (Philippines)
3rd Asian Games	1958	Tokyo (Japan)
4th Asian Games	1962	Jakarta (Indonesia)
5th Asian Games	1966	Bangkok (Thailand)
6th Asian Games	1970	Bangkok (Thailand)
7th Asian Games	1974	Teheran (Iran)
8th Asian Games	1978	Bangkok (Thailand)
9th Asian Games	1982	New Delhi (India)
10th Asian Games	1986	Seoul (Korea)
11th Asian Games	1990	Beijing (China)
12th Asian Games	1994	Hiroshima (Japan)
13th Asian Games	1998	Bangkok (Thailand)
14th Asian Games	2002	Bhusan
15th Asian Games	2006	Will be held at Doha

The First Asiad in New Delhi, India

The First Asian Games, originally scheduled for 1950, was postponed until March 1951 because of the delayed preparations. Four hundred and eighty-nine athletes from Afghanistan, Burma, India, Indonesia, Iran, Japan, Nepal, the Philippines, Singapore, SriLanka, and Thailand competed in athletics, aquatics, basketball, cycling, football and weightlifting in the eight-day Games from 4 March 1951 to 12 March 1951.

Details of the 1st Asian Games are given below:

Held at	New Delhi, March 04 to March 11, 1951
Participating Nations	11 countries/NOCs
Participants	500
Sports/Events :	Six Athletics, Swimming, Football, Cycling, Basketball & Weightlifting

Medals Tally

Rank	*Nation*	*G*	*S*	*B*	*Total*
1	Japan	24	20	14	58
2	India	15	18	19	52
3	Iran	8	5	2	15
4	Singapore	4	6	2	12
5	Philippines	3	5	7	15
6	Ceylon	-	1	-	1
7	Indonesia	-	-	5	5
8	Myanmar	-	-	3	3

Korea was unable to participate because of the Korean War. The first gold medalist was N.C. Kok of Singapore who won the 1500-meter freestyle swimming. Winning all four freestyle swimming events, he won four gold medals. Japan placed first with 24 gold medals, 20 silver medals and 14 bronze medals, followed by India which garnered 15 gold, 18 silver and 19 bronze medals. Japan had been barred from the London Olympics for initiating the Pacific War and was not invited to the founding meeting of AGF but was allowed to participate in the First Asian Games.

The Second Asiad in Manila, the Philippines

A total of 1,280 athletes from 18 countries participated in the nine-day Games from 1 May 1954 to 10 May 1954. The 18 participating countries included Cambodia, Hong Kong, Korea, Malaysia, North Borneo and Vietnam. Of the six sports events of the first Asian Games, cycling was dropped and boxing, shooting and wrestling were added to increase the number of sports to eight. Japan won first place garnering 38 gold, 36 silver and 24 bronze medals.

The host country, the Philippines, won second place with 14 gold, 14 silver and 17 bronze medals. Participating in Asain Games for the first time, Korea won third place with eight gold, six silver and five bronze medals.

Details of the 2st Asian Games are given below:

Held at	Manila, Philippines May 01 to May 09, 1954
Participating Nations	18
Participants	1,241
Sports/Events	Eight Athletics, Swimming, Soccer,Basketball, Weightlifting, Wrestling, Boxing & Shooting
Medals Tally:	

Rank	*Nation*	*G*	*S*	*B*	*Total*
1	Japan	38	36	24	98
2	Philippines	14	14	17	45
3	Korea	8	6	5	19
4	Pakistan	4	5	-	9
5	India	4	4	5	14
6	China	2	4	6	12
7	Myanmar	2	-	2	4
8	Israel	2	-	1	3
9	Singapore	1	3	4	8
10	Ceylon	-	1	1	2
11	Indonesia	-	-	3	3
12	Hong Kong	-	-	1	1

The Third Asiad in Tokyo, Japan

Details of the 3rd Asian Games are given below:

Held at	Tokyo, May 24 to June 01, 1958
Participating Nations	20
Participants	1,692
Sports/Events	13 Athletics, Swimming, Soccer,Basketball, Boxing, Wrestling,Weightlifting, Shooting, Tennis, Volleyball, Table Tennis, Hockey, and Cycling
Medals Tally	

The nine-day Third Asian Games were held from 24 May 1958 to 2 June 1958, with participation of 1,820 athletes from 20 countries who competed in 13 different sports consisting of the eight sports of the Second Asiad and tennis, volleyball, table tennis, hockey and cycling. Japan again won top place with 67 gold, 41 silver and 30 bronze medals, followed by the Philippines which won eight gold, 19 silver and 21 bronze medals. Korea dispatched a 156-man delegation to win third place with eight gold, 19 silver and 12 bronze medals. Lee Chang Hun of Korea won the marathon race.

Rank	*Nation*	*G*	*S*	*B*	*Total*
1	Japan	67	41	30	138
2	Philippines	8	19	21	48
3	Korea	8	7	12	27
5	China	6	9	10	25
5	Pakistan	6	5	4	15
6	India	5	3	3	11
7	Iran	4	6	6	16
8	Vietnam	2	-	-	2
9	Myanmar	2	-	-	2
10	Singapore	1	1	-	2
11	Ceylon	1	-	-	1
12	Indonesia	-	2	4	6
13	Thailand	-	1	3	4
14	Malaysia	-	-	2	2
15	Israel	-	-	1	1
16	Hong Kong	-	-	1	1

The Fourth Asiad in Jakarta, Indonesia

When the hosting country, Indonesia, opposed the participation of Chinese Taipei and Israel, the noble ideal of peace and friendship of the Asian Games was jeopardized. The IOC said that it would cancel its approval of the Jakarta Asian Games should the host country reject the two countries. The International Amateur Athletic Federation (IAAF) declared that unless the two countries were allowed to participate in the Jakarta Asiad, it would withdraw its approval of the Games and the athletes and their countries who participated would be disqualified as players and IAAF membership.

President of the International Weightlifting Federation (IWF) flew to Jakarta to warn that if the two countries were excluded from the Games the IWF would regard the Games as an unofficial and only a friendship meet. As Indonesia insisted on the exclusion of the two countries, the IWF expelled the Indonesian Weightlifting Federation and decided not to hold the weightlifting event in the Jakarta Asiad.

Without the participation of Chinese Taipei and Israel, 16 countries with 1,460 athletes competed in the 12-day Asian Games from 24 August 1962 to 5 August 1962. The 13 sports of the Games included badminton, which was played for the first time at the Games. Japan won first place with 73 gold, 56 silver and 23 bronze medals, followed by India which collected 10 gold, 13 silver and 10 bronze medals.

Details of the 4th Asian Games are given below:

Held at	Jakarta, Indonesia August 24 to September 04, 1962
Participating Nations	18
Participants	1,527
Sports/Events	13 Athletics, Swimming, Soccer, Tennis, Basketball, Volleyball, Table Tennis, Cycling, Boxing, Wrestling, Shooting, Hockey, and Badminton
Medals Tally	

Rank	Nation	G	S	B	Total
1	Japan	73	56	23	152
2	India	10	13	10	33
3	Indonesia	9	12	27	48
4	Philippines	7	4	16	27
5	Korea	4	4	7	15
6	Pakistan	3	4	4	11
7	Thailand	2	5	5	12
8	Malaysia	2	3	5	10
9	Myanmar	2	1	7	10
11	Singapore	1	-	1	2
12	Ceylon	-	1	2	3
13	Hong Kong	-	-	1	1

The Fifth Asiad in Bangkok, Thailand

Details of the 5th Asian Games are given below:

Held at	Bangkok, Thailand December 09 to December 20, 1966
Participating Nations	18
Participants	2,500
Sports/Events	14 Athletics, Swimming, Soccer,Tennis, Basketball, Volleyball, Table Tennis, Cycling, Boxing, Wrestling, Weightlifting, Shooting, Hockey, and Badminton
Medals Tally:	

Eighteen countries sent over 2,500 athletes and officials to the Fifth Asian Games, held between 9-20 December 1966, to compete in 14 different sports. Chinese Taipei and Israel returned to the Asian Games and Korea dispatched a 275-man delegation to compete in all 14 sports. During this Games, Korea was chosen to host the Sixth Asian Games in 1970. Japan again was the top winner garnering 78 gold, 53 silver and 33 bronze medals. Korea won second place for the first time in Asian Games with 12 gold, 18 silver and 21 bronze medals. Thailand, the host country, placed third with 12 gold, 14 silver and 11 bronze medals.

Rank	Nation	G	S	B	Total
1	Japan	78	53	33	164
2	Korea	12	18	21	51
3	Thailand	12	14	11	37
4	Malaysia	7	5	6	18
5	India	7	4	11	22
6	Indonesia	7	4	10	21
7	Iran	6	8	17	31
8	China	5	9	10	24
9	Israel	3	5	3	11
10	Philippines	2	15	25	42
11	Pakistan	2	4	2	8
12	Myanmar	1	-	4	5
13	Singapore	-	5	7	12
14	Vietnam	-	1	2	3
15	Ceylon	-	-	4	4
16	Hong Kong	-	-	1	1

The Sixth Asiad in Bangkok, Thailand

After Korea gave up hosting rights for the Sixth Asian Games because of domestic reasons, the Sixth Asiad was held in Bangkok, Thailand, with the financial support of Korea and a few other countries, for 12 days beginning 9

December 1970. Over 2,400 athletes from 18 countries participated in the Games which featured 13 sports. Tennis and table tennis were not played and yachting was included for the first time.

Details of the 6th Asian Games are given below:

Held at	Bangkok, Thailand December 09 to December 20, 1970
Participating Nations	18
Participants	2,500
Sports/Events	13 Athletics, Swimming, Soccer,Basketball, Volleyball, Cycling, Boxing, Wrestling, Weightlifting,Shooting, Hockey, Badminton and Sailing

Medals Tally:

Rank	Nation	G	S	B	Total
1	Japan	74	47	23	144
2	Korea	18	13	23	54
3	Thailand	9	17	13	39
4	Iran	9	7	7	23
5	India	6	9	10	25
6	Israel	6	6	5	17
7	Malaysia	5	1	7	13
8	Myanmar	3	2	7	12
9	Indonesia	2	5	17	24
10	Ceylon	2	2	-	4
11	Philippines	1	9	12	22
12	China	1	5	12	18
13	Pakistan	1	2	7	10
14	Singapore	-	6	9	15
15	Cambodia	-	2	3	5
16	Vietnam	-	-	2	2

Japan won 74 gold, 47 silver and 23 bronze medals to win first place. Korea won second place for the second consecutive Games with 18 gold, 13 silver and 23 bronze medals. Korea's Cho Oh Ryon won the 400-meter and 1500-meter freestyle swimming. Korea also won gold medals in men's high-board diving and women's shot put. Thailand followed Korea with 9 gold, 17 silver and 13 bronze medals.

THE SEVENTH ASIAD IN TEHRAN, IRAN

The expulsion of Chinese Taipei and Israel again haunted the Seventh Asian Games. About 10 months before the Seventh Asiad, the AGF General Assembly on 16 November 1973, expelled Chinese Taipei and admitted the D.P.R. Korea. Iran, the host country, despite the opposition of Arabic nations, allowed Israeli to participate in Asian Games. Communist bloc nations, such as the People's Republic of China, Mongolia and D.P.R Korea, took part in Asian Games for the first time. Both Korea and D.P.R Korea competed in the Games.

Details of the 7th Asian Games are given below:

Held at	Teheran, Iran, September 01 to September 16, 1974
Participating Nations	25
Participants	3,000
Sports/Events	16 Athletics, Swimming, Shooting, Cycling, Weightlifting, Gymnastics, Wrestling, Boxing, Table Tennis, Basketball, Volleyball, Soccer, Tennis, Badminton, Fencing, and Hockey
Medals Tally	

Arabic nations, D.P.R. Korea, Pakistan and the People's Republic of China refused to compete in tennis, fencing, basketball and football matches with Israel. Twenty-five countries sent 3,010 athletes to compete in 16 sports at the Seventh Asiad between 1-16 September 1974. Japan, again, won the most medals including 75 gold, 49 silver, and 51 bronze medals. Iran came forward to place second with 36 gold, 28 silver and 17 bronze medals. The People's Republic of China, a new comer, placed third, collecting 33 gold, 45 silver and 28 bronze medals.

Rank	*Nation*	*G*	*S*	*B*	*Total*
1	Japan	75	49	51	175
2	Iran	36	28	17	81
3	China	33	45	28	106

The Eight Asiad in Bangkok, Thailand

The Eighth Asian Games originally planned for Islamabad, Pakistan, was held in Bangkok, Thailand, as Pakistan gave up the rights to host the Games because of domestic reasons. Including the Eighth Asiad, Thailand hosted three Asian Games. Israel was expelled from the Asian Games and Syria was readmitted as a member of the Asian Games. United Arab Emirates, Bangladesh, Lebanon, Qatar and Saudi Arabia were newly admitted to Asian Games.

The Bangkok Asian Games Organizing Committee suddenly proposed to use the name of the Republic of Korea rather then Korea. At the last minute, just before the opening ceremony, the Organizing Committee decided to continue to use the name Korea. 3,842 athletes representing 25 countries compete in 19 different sports between 9-20 December 1978. Archery and bowling were new sports and yachting was revived in the Games. Japan ranked first garnering 70 gold, 58 silver and 49 bronze medals.

Details of the 8th Asian Games are given below:

Held at	Bangkok, Thailan December 09 to December 20, 1978
Participating Nations	27
Participants	4,000
Sports/Events	19 Athletics, Swimming, Soccer, Tennis, Basketball, Volleyball, Table Tennis, Cycling, Boxing, Wrestling, Weightlifting, Fencing, Shooting, Gymnastics, Hockey, Badminton, Archery, Bowling and Sailing

Medals Tally

Rank	*Nation*	*G*	*S*	*B*	*Total*
1	Japan	70	58	49	177
2	China	51	55	45	151
3	South Korea	18	20	31	69
4	North Korea	15	13	15	43
5	Thailand	11	11	20	42
6	India	11	11	6	28
7	Indonesia	8	7	18	33
8	Pakistan	4	4	9	17
9	Philippines	4	4	6	14
10	Iraq	2	4	6	12
11	Singapore	2	1	4	7
12	Malaysia	2	1	3	6
13	Mongolia	1	3	5	9
14	Lebanon	1	1	-	2
15	Syria	1	-	-	1
16	Myanmar	-	3	3	6
17	Hong Kong	-	2	3	5
18	Sri Lanka	-	-	2	2
19	Kuwait	-	-	1	1

The People's Republic of China followed Japan with 51 gold, 20 silver and 45 bronze medals. Korea won third place, winning 18 gold, 20 silver and 31 bronze medals and D.P.R. Korea placed fourth with 15 gold, 13 silver and 15 bronze medals.

THE NINTH ASIAD IN NEW DELHI, INDIA

The Ninth Asian Games in New Delhi, 19 November through 4 December 1982, was the first Asian Games under the control of the OCA. The AGF, under whose jurisdiction the first eight Asian Games had been held, dissolved to make way for the OCA. 4,595 athletes representing 33 countries competed in 21 sports. The number of the participating countries was the greatest in Asian Games history. Handball, equestrian sports, rowing and golf were played for the first time in Asian Games history. Fencing and bowling were not included in the 21 events of the Ninth Asiad.

Details of the 9th Asian Games are given below:

Held at	New Delhi, India November 19 to December 04, 1982
Participating Nations	33
Participants	4,500
Sports/Events	21 Athletics, Swimming, Soccer, Tennis, Basketball, Volleyball, Table Tennis, Handball, Cycling, Boxing, Wrestling, Weightlifting, Archery, Shooting, Equestrian, Gymnastics, Hockey, Badminton, Canoeing, Sailing , Golf
Medals Tally	

Garnering 61 gold, 51 silver, and 41 bronze medals, the People's Republic of China replaced Japan, which won 57 gold, 52 silver, and 44 bronze medals, as the winner of the first place during the Ninth Asian Games. Korea placed third with 28 gold, 28 silver, and 37 bronze medals, followed by D.P.R. Korea with 17 gold, 19 silver, and 20 bronze medals. Host of the tenth Asiad in 1986 and the 24th Olympiad in 1988, Korea participated in the Ninth Asian Games with a 406-man delegation and an observation team to study the facilities, management and sports events.

Rank	Nation	G	S	B	Total
1	China	61	51	41	153
2	Japan	57	52	44	153
3	South Korea	28	28	37	93
4	North Korea	17	19	20	56
5	India	13	19	25	57
6	Indonesia	4	4	7	15
7	Iran	4	4	4	12
8	Pakistan	3	3	5	11
9	Mongolia	3	3	1	7
10	Philippines	2	3	9	14
11	Iraq	2	3	4	9
12	Thailand	1	5	4	10
13	Kuwait	1	3	3	7
14	Syria	1	1	1	3
15	Malaysia	1	-	3	4
16	Singapore	1	-	2	3
17	Afghanistan	-	1	-	1
18	Lebanon	-	-	1	1
19	Bahrain	-	-	1	1
20	Hong Kong	-	-	1	1
21	Qatar	-	-	1	1
22	Vietnam	-	-	1	1

The Tenth Asiad in Seoul, Korea

The tenth Asian Games was held in Seoul, Korea, from September 20 to October 5, 1986, with 3,345 athletes (755 women) from 27 countries and regions participating. There were 269 events in 25 sports, with judo and taekwondo as newly added sports. 83 Asian records and 3 world records were broken and 2 world records were equalled. Attending the opening ceremony were the Korean president, the Japanese prime minister, the OCA president Sheikh Fahad Al Sabah, the IOC president Juan Antonio Samaranch and officials from various international sports organizations. The tenth Asian Games to be held in Seoul, so sports facilities, stadiums and gymnasiums were all constructed according to the requirements of the Olympic Games.

Details of the 10th Asian Games are given below:

Held at	Seoul, Korea September 20 to October 05, 1986
Participating Nations	27
Participants	4,839
Sports/Events	25
	Athletics, Swimming, Archery, Badminton, Basketball, Bowling, Boxing, Cycling, Equestrian, Golf, Fencing, Soccer, Judo, Hockey, Gymnastics, Handball, Canoeing, Shooting, Table Tennis, Tennis, Taekwondo, Volleyball,
Wrestling, Weightlifting and	
	Yacht Racing
Medals Tally	

China sent 385 athletes to participate in 20 sports and won 94 gold medals, holding sway over Asia for the second time. The Indian woman athletic star P.T. Usha won 4 firsts, becoming the biggest winner of gold medals in athletics. Hamada Ahmad from Bahrain defeated his Japanese opponent and Won a gold medal in men 400m hurdle. Hong Kong bowling player Chen Ju Hong Won the first gold medal for Hong Kong in the history of the Asiad. Chinese gymnast Li Ning won 4 gold medals and silver medals, becoming the biggest winner of medals at the Games. Japanese hammer player Murobushi Shgenobu became champion for the fifth successive time since the sixth Asian Games.

Rank	Nation	G	S	B	Total
1	China	94	82	46	222
2	South Korea	93	55	76	224
3	Japan	58	76	77	211
4	Iran	6	6	10	22
5	India	5	9	23	37
6	Philippines	4	5	9	18
7	Thailand	3	10	13	26
8	Pakistan	2	3	4	9
9	Indonesia	1	5	4	10
10	Hong Kong	1	1	3	5
11	Qatar	1	-	3	4
12	Lebanon	1	-	1	2
13	Bahrain	1	-	1	2
14	Malaysia	-	5	5	10
15	Iraq	-	5	2	7
16	Jordan	-	3	1	4
17	Kuwait	-	1	7	8
18	Singapore	-	1	4	5
19	Saudi Arabia	-	1	-	1
20	Nepal	-	-	8	8
21	Bangladesh	-	-	1	1
22	Oman	-	-	1	1

The Eleventh Asiad in Beijing, China

The 11th Asian Games was held from September 22 to October 7 in 1990 in Beijing, the capital of China, with the motto "unity, friendship and progress". Participating were 4,655 athletes (1,462 women) from 37 countries and regions. There were 308 events in 27 sports, with softball, sepak takraw, wushu, kabaddi and rowing as newly-added sports, and baseball and soft tennis as demonstration sports.

With the largest number of sports ever seen in the Asiad, the 11th Asian Games was the first large scale international sports meet to be held in the history of China. 7 world records were bettered, 89 Asian records broken, 189 Asian Games records and one world record, 11 Asian records and 20 Asian Games records were equalled.

Details of the 11th Asian Games are given below:

Held at	Beijing, China September 22 to October 07, 1990
Participating Nations	37 (All OCA members except Iraq and Jordan)
Participants	6,122
Sports/Events	27 Athletics, Swimming, Archery, Badminton, Basketball, Boxing, Canoeing, Kabaddi, Cycling, Golf, Fencing, Soccer, Handball, Judo, Gymnastics, Hockey, Canoeing, Sepak Takraw, Shooting, Softball, Table Tennis, Tennis, Volleyball,Weightlifting, Wrestling, Wushu, and Sailing
Medals Tally	

Rank	Nation	G	S	B	Total
1	China	183	107	51	341
2	South Korea	54	54	73	181
3	Japan	38	60	76	174
4	North Korea	12	31	39	82
5	Iran	4	6	8	18
6	Pakistan	4	1	7	12
7	Indonesia	3	6	21	30
8	Qatar	3	2	1	6
9	Thailand	2	7	8	17
10	Malaysia	2	2	4	8
11	India	1	8	14	23
12	Mongolia	1	7	9	17
13	Philippines	4	5	9	18
14	Syria	1	-	2	3
15	Oman	1	-	-	1
16	Chinese Taipei	-	10	21	31
17	Hong Kong	-	2	5	7
18	Sri Lanka	-	2	1	3
18	Singapore	-	1	4	5
19	Bangladesh	-	1	-	1
20	Myanmar	-	-	1	1
21	Laos	-	-	1	1
22	Macau	-	-	1	1
21	Nepal	-	-	1	1
22	Saudi Arabia	-	-	1	1

The Twelveth Asiad in Hiroshima, Japan

The 12th Games in Hiroshima, with the participation of 6828 athletes and official from 42 NOCs, including five

Central Asian countries newly independent from the former Soviet Union, and featuring 34 sports, broke the Beijing records and became the largest event ever in the history of the Asian Games.

Details of the 12th Asian Games are given below:

Held at	Hiroshima, Japan October 02 to October 16, 1994
Participating Nations	42
Participants	6,824
Sports/Events	34 Athletics, Swimming, Archery, Badminton, Baseball, Basketball, Bowling, Boxing, Canoeing, Cycling, Equestrian, Fencing, Soccer, Golf, Gymnastics, Handball, Hockey, Judo, Kabaddi, Karatedo, Rowing, Modern Pentathlon, Sepak Takraw, Shooting, Softball, Table Tennis, Taekwondo, Tennis, Volleyball, Weightlifting, Wrestling, Wushu, and Sailing

Medals Tally

Rank	Nation	G	S	B	Total
1	China	125	83	58	266
2	Japan	64	75	79	218
3	South Korea	63	56	64	183
4	Kazakhstan	25	26	26	77
5	Uzbekistan	10	11	19	40
6	Iran	9	9	8	26
7	Chinese Taipei	7	12	24	31

8	India	4	3	15	22
9	Malaysia	4	2	13	19
10	Qatar	4	1	15	20
11	Indonesia	3	12	11	26
12	Thailand	3	9	13	25
13	Syria	3	3	1	7
14	Philippines	3	2	8	13
15	Kuwait	3	1	5	9
16	Saudi Arabia	1	3	5	9
17	Turkmenistan	1	3	3	7
18	Mongolia	1	2	6	9
19	Singapore	1	1	5	7
20	Vietnam	1	2	-	3
21	Hong Kong	-	5	7	12
22	Pakistan	-	4	6	10
23	Kyrgyzstan	-	4	5	9
24	Jordan	-	2	2	4
25	U. Arab Emirate	-	1	3	4
26	Macau	-	1	1	2
27	Sri Lanka	-	1	1	2
28	Bangladesh	-	1	-	1
29	Brunei	-	-	2	2
30	Myanmar	-	-	2	2
31	Nepal	-	-	2	2
32	Tajikistan	-	-	2	2

The 13th Asian Games

The 13th Asian Games was held from Dec 6 to Dec 20, 1998 at Bangkok. This is the largest Asian Games to he held in this millennium, with 9,469 athletes and officials from over 41 countries participating. The Games went smoothly without any major problem in the spirit of the motto: Friendship Beyond Frontiers.

Details of the 13th Asian Games are given below:

Held at	Hiroshima, Japan October December 06 to December 20,
1998	
Participating Nations	41
Participants	9,699
Sports/Events	36
	Athletics, Archery, Badminton, Baseball, Basketball, Billiard, Golf, Bowling, Boxing, Canoeing, Cycling, Equestrian, Fencing, Soccer, Judo, Gymnastics, Handball, Hockey, Kabaddi, Karatedo, Rowing, Rugby, Sepak Takraw, Shooting, Softball, Soft Tennis, Squash, Swimming, Table Tennis, Tennis, Taekwondo, Volleyball, Wrestling, Wushu, Weightlifting and Sailing

Medals Tally

Rank	Nation	G	S	B	Total
1	China	129	78	67	274
2	South Korea	65	46	53	164
3	Japan	52	61	68	181
4	Thailand	24	26	40	90
4	Kazakhstan	24	24	30	78
5	Taipei	19	17	41	77
6	Iran	10	11	13	34
7	North Korea	7	14	12	33
8	India	7	11	17	35
9	Uzbekistan	6	22	12	40
10	Indonesia	6	10	11	27
11	Malaysia	5	10	14	29
12	Hong Kong	5	6	6	17
13	Kuwait	4	6	4	14
14	Sri Lanka	3	0	3	6
15	Pakistan	2	4	9	15

16	Singapore	2	3	9	14
17	Qatar	2	3	3	8
18	Mongolia	2	2	10	14
19	Myanmar	1	6	4	11
20	Philippines	1	5	12	18
21	Vietnam	1	5	11	17
22	Turkmenistan	1	0	1	2
23	Kyrgyzstan	-	3	3	6
24	Jordan	-	3	2	5
25	Syria	-	2	4	6
26	Nepal	-	1	3	4
27	U. Arab Emirate	-	1	1	2
28	Macau	-	1	-	1
29	Bangladesh	-	-	1	1
30	Brunei	-	-	1	1
31	Laos	-	-	1	1
32	Oman	-	-	1	1

14th Asiad in Busan, South Korea

The 14th Asian Games held at Busan (South Korea) from 29th September to 14th October, 2002. Taking more than a third of all gold medals on offer at the Busan Asian Games, world sports power China demonstrated once again it has grown beyond Asia. China was just too strong a competitor for other Asian countries, including the distant runner-up South Korea and third place holder Japan.

Beginning with two fencing golds won on the Sept. 29, the opening day of the 16-day meet, athletes from the world's most populous country swept the board. China's medal haul comprises 150 gold, 84 silver and 74 bronze medals. The feat was no surprise for other participants as the unrivaled athletic power has dominated Asian sports for about two decades. In the previous Bangkok games in 1998, the country also took home more than a third of all golds on offer, 129 of 378, to be exact.

Most participants, and China itself, took it for granted the reigning champion would take the most medals this time too. Finishing first in the medal tally was not the first goal for China. The country had openly stated it would use this year's games to develop stars and better the quality of gold medals in preparation for the 2004 Athens Olympics and the 2008 Olympics on home soil. To that purpose the country picked young athletes, with an average age of 23.3 years. In addition some 80 percent of the athletes have not experienced competing at either Asiad or Olympics level.

Details of the 13th Asian Games are given below:

Held at	Busan (South Korea), 29th September to 14th October, 2002
Participating Nations	44
Participants	9782
Sports/Events	38 Archery, Athletics, Badminton, Baseball, Basketball, Billiard & Snooker, Bowling, Boxing, Canoeing, Cycling, Equestrian, Fencing, Soccer, Golf, Gymnastics, Handball, Hockey, Judo, Kabaddi, Karatedo, Rowing, Rugby, Sepaktakraw, Shooting, Softball, soft Tennis, Squash, Swimming, Table Tennis, Taekwondo, Tennis, Volleyball, Weightlifting, Wrestling, Wushu, Modern Pentathlon, Sailing and Body Building
Medals Tally	

Many teenage star athletes were discovered, ncluding female gymnast Zhang Nan, male gymnast Teng Haibin, female weightlifter Liu Chunhong, female shooter Du Li and female swimmer Qi Hui. Considering their youth, they are expected to play a key role in Chinese sports for the next 10 years. In addition to individual events China also succeeded in upgrading its performance in ball sports. While maintaining its traditional edge in basketball and volleyball, the country also made big strides in hockey and handball, posing serious challenges to South Korea which has dominated these sports in the past. China also succeeded in bettering the qualify of its golds. This year's Asiad saw a total of 22 world records with 17 of them set by Chinese athletes. More encouraging is that most of China's new world record holders are in their teens or early twenties. Host South Korea and its rival Japan fought hard for the second spot in the medal standings, but are still far behind China whose gold medals outnumbers their combined total of number one awards. Kazakhstan stood fourth with 20 golds. India and Saudi Arabia stood out in athletics, posing serious challenges to China and Japan.

Rank	Nation	G	S	B	Total
1	China	150	84	74	308
2	Korea	96	80	84	260
3	Japan	44	74	72	190
4	Kazakhstan	20	26	30	76
5	Uzbekistan	15	12	24	51
6	Thailand	14	19	10	43
7	Taipei	10	17	25	52
8	India	10	12	13	35
9	D.P.R. Korea	9	11	13	33
10	Iran	8	14	14	36
11	Saudi Arabia	7	1	1	9
12	Malaysia	6	8	16	30
13	Singapore	5	2	10	17
14	Indonesia	4	7	12	23
15	Vietnam	4	7	7	18

16	Hong Kong	4	6	11	21
17	Qatar	4	5	8	17
18	Philippines	3	7	16	26
19	Bahrain	3	2	2	7
20	Kyrgyzstan	2	4	6	12
21	Kuwait	2	1	5	8
22	Sri Lanka	2	1	3	6
23	Pakistan	1	6	6	13
24	Myanmar	1	5	6	12
25	Turkmenistan	1	2	1	4
26	Mongolia	1	1	12	14
27	Lebanon	1	-	-	1
28	Tajikistan	-	2	4	6
29	Macau	-	2	2	4
30	U.A. E	-	2	1	3
31	Bangladesh	-	1	-	1
32	Syria	-	-	3	3
32	Nepal	-	-	3	3
34	Laos	-	-	2	2
34	Jordan	-	-	2	2
36	Afghanistan	-	-	1	1
36	Yemen	-	-	1	1
36	Brunei	-	-	1	1
36	Palestine	-	-	1	1

14TH ASIAD IN DOHA

15th Asian Games will be held at Doha in the year 2006. The State of Qatar and its capital city, Doha, have been selected, after an intense competition with major Asian cities, to host the games from 1st to 15th December, 2006. The Doha Asian Games Organising Committee (DAGOC) and the Qatar National Olympic Committee have shared the responsibilities of organising these meetings.

Around 300 delegates from the 45 member countries of the OCA are expected to attend. Various issues related to the Doha Asian Games will be discussed, and the host of the 2010 Asian Games will be officially revealed.

5

Afro Asian Games

The Afro Asian games were first proposed in 1983, but attempts to hold Afro Asian Games in 1985, 1991, 1999 and 2001 all had fallen through. India, at the very least, should be given credit for their perseverance in bringing the 2003 Afro Asian Games to their beginning.

The first mention of a competition for the combined continents of Africa and Asia was in April of 1983, when Olympic Review stated that Afro Asian Games would be held in New Delhi. In December, 1983, Olympic Review noted that the proposed games venue had been changed to Kuwait and would be held in 1985.

The games were to combine the four best teams in basketball, football and handball, the four best track athletes in each event and the two best boxers in each weight class, from each region, Africa and Asia.

In April 1985 the games were still on but in September they were cancelled, the organizers citing political instability.

In 1989 the idea resurfaced once again with the announcement that New Delhi would host the games in November 1991. Once again nothing came of the plans.

The idea was brought to life again at the end of the and Afro Asian games were to be held in Pune, India in 1999, then New Delhi in November of 1999. These games were not cancelled but were postponed until November 2001. Preparations were slow however, and this, combined with the terrorist attacks in the United States in September 2001 caused the games to be postponed indefinitely once again.

Egypt had been mentioned as a tentative host for 2005, if the games had been held successfully in 2001, but plans for a second edition have been put on hold until after a first edition is successfully held.

In May of 2002, India proposed holding the Afro Asian Games in Hyderabad, in 2003. Hyderabad was chosen because facilities had recently been upgraded for India's national games.

IST AFRO ASIAN GAMES, HYDERABAD, INDIA

The Ist ever Afro Asian Games were held in Hyderabad, the Capital of Andhra Pradesh State in India from 24th of October to 1st November, 2003. President OCA presided over the Opening Ceremony of the Ist Afro Asian Games. The games were opened by the Deputy Prime Minister of India Mr. L.K. Advani.

A brilliantly conceptualised display of colour and gaiety marked the grand Opening Ceremony, which got the first-ever Afro Asian Games under way at the GMC Balayogi Stadium in Gachibowli on the outskirts of Hyderabad. The ceremony had all the pomp and grandeur befitting the important occasion, which added a new chapter to the sports history of this city. The whole show was designed to encapsulate the huge variety of culture and traditions of the two continents and it managed to fulfil this demanding task fairly successfully.

To coordinate the various dances, acrobatics and the display of martial arts by such a large number of participants was truly a mind-boggling feat and the organisers deserve praise for putting up the show in such a precise manner. There were no major hitches or glitches and the programme was gone through smoothly, adding to its grandeur. The most breathtaking and remarkable aspect of the show was the fusion of colour, music and lights, which lit up the entire stadium and sent the audience into raptures.

Spotted among the audience were some of the best known personalities of the Hindi and Telugu film industry such as Sanjay Dutt, Chiranjeevi and Balakrishna, while from the world of sports, tennis star Leander Paes and Mohd. Azharuddin were among the more prominent faces.

To top it all, India's hopes of hosting the Commonwealth Games got a boost when Sheikh Al Fahad Ahmed Al Sabah, President of the Olympic Council of Asia, endorsed India's initiative. The visiting VIPs seemed to have been impressed by the organisational ability and commitment towards sports that they witnessed in India and the mood was upbeat during the opening ceremony. In his speech, N. Chandrababu Naidu, Chief Minister of Andhra Pradesh, made it clear that his government was willing and ready to host more such sports extravaganzas, including the Commonwealth Games and the Olympics if given the chance.

The opening ceremony succeeded in showcasing the rich traditions and culture of the host State and the country, and also sent out a message to the world at large that the host was capable of conducting major events in a splendid manner. An unusual aspect of the march past was that the players trooped into the stadium in two groups – Africans and Asians, and not in a countrywise order. The informal manner made the march-past look more like a closing ceremony rather than the inaugural one. One felt that perhaps the move to club the participants into two continentwise groups, instead of the usual practice of each country's team marching separately under its own banner, was due to the fact that there was not enough representation from each country to make up sizeable contingents in the march past. The opening of the centre-stage, which was shaped like a lotus flower, was quite spectacular and the rendition of the Atha Swagatam song by S. P. Balasubramaniam and Usha along with 200 children and 300 Kuchipudi dancers set the right spirit combining the mood of sobriety and gaiety in proper proportions.

When it came to addressing the gathering, one felt the speakers should have restricted themselves to the bare minimum on an occasion like this. The audience became a little restive at this stage and so also the players, some of whom were seen leaving the arena in small groups and this could have been avoided. The Chief Minister Chandrababu Naidu's suggestion to the visitors to try out the taste of Hyderabadi biryani and buy Hyderabad's world famous pearls met with enthusiastic and loud response from the audience.

The honour of lighting the torch was given to Karnam Malleswari, winner of the bronze medal in the Sydney Olympic Games. Triple Olympian hockey player Mukesh Kumar and Malleswari took the torch up to the final point and then Malleswari ascended the stage to set it alight. This was followed by a spectacular display of lights and fireworks, which lit up the surroundings for miles, well beyond the confines of the stadium.

The display of martial arts namely Kalaripayattu, Thangta and Kung Fu was breathtaking. The participants showed their expertise and the movements were superbly done with grace. Also a grand sight was the depiction of the battle of Kalinga by about 1000 participants. The acting out of Mahatma Gandhi's famous Dandi march and the speech on the giant screen by former South African President Nelson Mandela brought to life the philosophy of freedom and equality and the deeds of the freedom fighters of these two countries. Film stars Mahima Choudhary, Simran and Urmila Matondkar regaled the audience with their dances and finally Shankar Mahadevan and others brought the show to an end with the rendition of the theme song.

A total of 2,000 athletes and officials from almost 75 countries of Asia and Africa participated in the Ist Afro Asian Games held from 24th October to 1st November, 2003.

Two World Records were broken - One in Shooting by Ms. Olga Dovgun from Kazakhstan in 50 M Rifle Prone (Women) who shot 600/600. The second was in Weightlifting by Ms. Sun Dan from China who lifted 277.5 Kgs in over 75 Kgs. in women categories.

China with 25 Gold, 11 Silver and 5 Bronze was placed first in Medals Tally and India with 19 Gold, 32 Silver and 29 bronze was placed second.

Hyderabad hosted the first Afro Asian Games, which saw delegates and dignitaries from over 120 countries representing Asia, Africa and few commonwealth countries. Players from 98 countries take part in eight disciplines namely Athletics, Boxing Football, Hockey, Shooting, Swimming, Tennis, and weightlifting.

The games were held at The GMC Balayogi Athletic Stadium,The Lal Bahadur Stadium,The Shooting Range, Hyderabad Central University,The Acquatics Complex, GMC Balayogi Stadium,The Tennis Complex, Fatehmaidan,The Kotla Vijayabhaskara Reddy Indoor Stadium. The games were being organised by Government of India,Government of Andhra Pradesh,Indian Olympic Association and Afro Asian Games Council.

The games were held over the Indian holiday period of Diwali (analogous in some respect to holding a games over the Christmas Period in North America or Europe) which was criticized by some. In addition, the Muslim period of Ramadan began during the games.

The intent of the Afro Asian Games was to reward the top four finishing teams and individuals from the 2002 Asian Games and the 2003 African Games, and have them meet head to head. In practice this turned out to be quite difficult to achieve.

Stars of the games were Sania Mirza, an Indian junior tennis player ranked in the 400s worldwide, who picked up four gold medals, in women's singles, women's doubles, mixed doubles, and for the women's team competition.

Japanese swimmers picked up numerous medals, Mizuki Wakabayashi with four gold medals, Takamitsu Kojima and Genki Imamura with three each.

China's Sun Dan from China, broke a world record in the women over 75 kilo category by lifting 168.5 kilos in the clean and jerk.

A surprise for Afro Asian Games organizers was the arrival of Namibian champion sprinter Frankie Fredericks, who, it was reported after the African Games, was retiring. Fredericks stated that he had been misunderstood and that he had only said that the Abuja Games were his final African Games, but he is not yet retiring! Frederick's would be 40 years old the next time the African Games are scheduled to roll around in 2007. Fredericks, took the 100 and 200 meter gold medals in Hyderabad, saying that he wanted to support the inaugural games and hoped that other athletes would support future Afro Asian events.

On a continental level, Asia won 82 gold, 80 silver and 88 bronze medals while Africa won 49 gold, 41 silver and 66 bronze medals. On a country basis, China, India, Japan, Nigeria and South Africa led the medals table.

A comparison of India's performance at the 2002 Asian Games and the 2003 Afro Asian Games proves how valuable it is to host a games. In the 2002 Asian Games, with 44 nations and 38 sports, India won 10 gold, 12 silver and 13 bronze medals, or 35 out of a total of 1350 medals awarded at those games about 2.6 percent of the medals. In the 2003 Afro Asian Games, with just 8 sports, and 406 medals, Indian athletes won 80 total medals, or 19.7 percent.

Closing Ceremony

The closing ceremony, began with a demonstration by jet fighters from the Indian Air Force, then a mixture of African and Asian cultural performances, with singers and dancers from India led by Remo Fernandes, Umoja of South Africa, Imperial State circus of China, Lebanese singer Diana Hadad, and Egyptian singer Hisham Abbas. The newly established Afro Asian Games council has announced that the next Games will be held in 2007 in Africa, with Nigeria, South Africa and Egypt being considered as hosts. A decision is preliminary scheduled to be made by the Association Of National Olympic Committees of Africa (ANOCA) in the next few months.

Medals Tally

Continent wise Medals Tally

Continent	Gold	Silver	Bronze	Total
Asia	82	80	88	245
Africa	49	51	66	166
Overall Total	131	131	149	411

Country wise Medals Tally

Country	Gold	Silver	Bronze	Total
China	25	11	5	41
India	19	32	29	80
Japan	15	6	2	23
Nigeria	10	12	13	35
South Africa	10	11	15	36
Korea	7	6	11	24
Algeria	7	6	9	22
Uzbekistan	7	2	3	12
Combined Africa	6	4	0	10
Kazakhstan	5	8	6	19
Ethiopia	5	5	3	13
Sudan	3	3	0	6
Iran	2	3	1	6
Kenya	2	0	3	5
Philippines	1	4	10	15
Egypt	1	1	4	6
Seychelles	1	1	2	4
Combined Africa 2	1	1	0	2
Namibia	1	0	2	3
Tanzania	1	0	1	2
Cameroon	1	0	1	2
Vietnam	1	0	0	1
Senegal	0	6	3	9
Thailand	0	2	6	8
Pakistan	0	2	1	3
Indonesia	0	2	1	3
Burkina Faso	0	1	0	1
Qatar	0	1	0	1
Tajikistan	0	1	0	1
Zimbabwe	0	0	5	5
Uganda	0	0	3	3
Sri Lanka	0	0	3	3
Malaysia	0	0	2	2
Chinese Taipei	0	0	2	2
Congo	0	0	1	1
Mongolia	0	0	1	1
Libya	0	0	1	1
Overall Total	131	131	149	411

Sports wise Medals Tally

Sport	Gold	Silver	Bronze	Total
Athletics	42	42	42	126
Swimming	38	38	38	114
Shooting	15	15	15	45
Weightlifting	15	15	15	45
Boxing	11	11	22	44
Tennis	7	7	14	28
Hockey	2	2	2	6
Football	1	1	1	3
Overall Total	131	131	149	411

A grand finale, which comprised a breathtaking display of colour and lights, marked the closing ceremony of the first Afro Asian Games in Hyderabad. The ceremony, which was well co-ordinated, exhibited a variety of cultures. Although there were a few common elements between the opening and closing ceremonies, this aspect could be overlooked for the whole show made a good impact and brought the curtains down in a befitting manner.

The President A.P.J. Abdul Kalam declared the Games closed and several dignitaries and sports administrators were at hand to grace the occasion. They included Suresh Kalmadi, IOA President, Randhir Singh, OCA Secretary General, Alfa Ibrahim Diallo, President of the Associated National Olympic Committees of Africa, Vikram Verma, Union Minister for Sports and of course the man whose initiative made everything possible N. Chandrababu Naidu, Chief Minister of Andhra Pradesh.

The CM drew a round of applause when he made a fervent plea for India to make a strong bid to host the Olympics and said that Hyderabad was ready to be the venue for this mega event. But all said and done, one felt that the speeches could have been restricted to the minimum on such an occasion.

The fireworks display was truly remarkable and lit up the night sky. Anchor Yukta Mukhi, former beauty queen did a commendable job and the cultural segments were interesting, particularly the acrobatics by the State circus of China. The songs rendered by singers such as Diana Haddad and Hisham Abbas brought the ambience of the deserts to the city of Hyderabad. India's own singers such as Hariharan and Remo Fernandes provided the Indian touch to the programme and regaled the audience. But the surprising aspect was the paltry number of sportspersons who were available to take part in the closing march past.

Generally at the closing ceremony of an event such as this, the march past on the final day will find the sportspersons in a relaxed mood after having gone through all the stress and tension of the sports tournaments. The participants have a chance to relax and mingle with each other and interact with the spectators. The festive atmosphere, usually witnessed during the closing ceremonies, provided a feeling of emotional bonding and friendship. So it was surprising to see just a handful of sportspersons trooping into the stadium and marching past the dais. Many of the participants had already left the venue it was learnt and this was the reason behind the poor turn out. This was something, which could have been avoided with a better planning.

Another aspect that disappointed many sports lovers was the mismanagement of the issuing of complimentary passes and tickets for the closing ceremony. Hundreds of genuine ticket holders were refused entry into the stadium by securitymen manning the gates. The reason being that the stadium was already full and there was no more space to accommodate the ticket holders. Many of them had come from faraway places but had to return home disappointed. To add injury to insult some were roughed up by the securitymen. They left the venue with bitter feelings that they had been cheated of their money. They had come with the hope of viewing the closing finale of what was one of the most magnificent sports events ever held in Hyderabad but their hopes were dashed. This was the major blemish to an otherwise well-conceived ending to a thrilling sports extravaganza.

It is now futile to examine whether the country deserved such an expensive inaugural Afro Asian Games. What must be assessed dispassionately is the efficacy of the venture and the degree of sporting excellence displayed during those eventful days in Hyderabad. Even assuming that the contests were mediocre and lacked world class fare, the fact that India cornered as many as 80 medals, more than what the super power of the region, China, could aggregate must be acknowledged.

China did top the gold medal tally with 25, but India picked up 19 with 32 silver and 29 bronze. Statistically speaking, as many as 35 countries from the two continents figured on the medal board, and India's second place on it makes the effort noteworthy. True, the big names were missing in some disciplines like soccer, athletics and shooting, but these aberrations should not cloud what the Indians had achieved, nor be dismissed as worthless. The golds, in men's and women's hockey, testified the level of competence. While the men prevailed over Pakistan twice in a space of four days to take the top honours, the women outclassed two major powers, South Korea and South Africa.

In the individual events, stars who were expected to strike it rich performed with a measure of credit. Anju George, Neelam Jaswant Singh in athletics and Anjali Bhagwat in shooting are worthy of being named as outstanding in the meet. Competition in athletics acquired a trace of class with the participation of Frankie Fredericks of Namibia and a few world level stars in long distance running from Ethiopia. The Chinese women lifters enhanced the stature of the competition what with San Dan breaking the world record in an event in which the home team's star performer, Karnam Malleswari, was missing, after taking part in the opening ceremony.

Viewed from a larger perspective of globalisation and the role of India as an all round developing power, the inaugural Afro Asian Games can be categorised as pathbreaking. Indisputably, the hiccups before the Games became a reality were far too many, genuine and created, more often the latter. Conceived as an instrument to strengthen the bonds between two large continents sometime in the late Eighties, it was difficult to convince many in the power hierarchy over the need for such a venture. Initially, it did look as though the chief proponent of the idea, the Indian Olympic Association, mishandled the whole project by making far too many commitments to crystallise the concept. But looking back, one should not flinch from paying a tribute to the persistence, patience and pragmatism of Suresh Kalmadi as head of the IOA.

Several hurdles had to be crossed and so many power brokers had to be silenced before he struck a rapport with the Chief Minister of Andhra Pradesh, Chandrababu Naidu, whose wholesome support ensured the creation of a magnificent infrastructure for the Games. No effort was spared by the Government to get the venues ready. The hockey administration headed by the FIH President, Els van Breda Vriesmann, was amazed by the fact that two artificial pitches were laid in less than three weeks time.

The optimism expressed by Suresh Kalmadi that the launch of the Afro Asian Games is a sure sign of framing a long chain to make sport a vibrant social, economic and political plank in the two continents is certainly not misplaced. He was not tired of citing the fact that it was India that gave shape to the dream of sportsmen and women through the first Asian Games in New Delhi in 1951 and how this idea caught the imagination of the youth to the point of staging as many as 14 successive Asiads without a break. One hopes that the fire lit in Hyderabad is kept burning in future with Africa taking up the gigantic task of hosting the second edition in 2007.

When the project was put up for approval, the International Olympic Committee, headed by the then President, Juan Antonio Samaranch, applauded it as a major promotional exercise. The present administration is unlikely to have any other opinion. But the delegates representing Asia and Africa in the IOC should endeavour to exercise their influence to get the event a greater recognition in future. After all, the two continents represent more than a majority of the global population thirsting for better conditions of living and dreaming of courting excellence using sport as the medium.

Whatever be the initial misgivings, the Afro Asian Games mirrored the fact that India has the wherewithal and expertise to stage a mega event with eclat.

India's Achievement in Afro Asian Games

Amidst the general mediocrity that various disciplines presented in the Afro Asian Games, athletics salvaged some pride for the Indian Olympic Association (IOA) and the host State with a few big names making it to Hyderabad. Of course it could have been a world-class fare had all the top stars made it. But then such an eventuality was never really on, despite the projections, promises and claims.

The very fact that Indians were able to win five gold medals in such a championship should tell its own tale. This is not to take any credit away from those who won the gold medals, discus thrower Anil Kumar and shot putter Shakti Singh in the men's section, and long jumper Anju George, discus thrower Neelam J. Singh and heptathlete J. J. Shobha in the women's section. At least in the case of Neelam, she can claim with some pride and satisfaction that she had recorded a season best of 61.94m to claim the gold in a field that included all those who mattered from either continent. Though the same could not have been said of the other events where the Indians gained gold and lesser medals, they can as well counter that it was not their fault that the big names stayed away from this meet.

The world-class fare many people talked about came only in a few events; in a majority of the events the performance levels were below our own National records. The oft-repeated argument that the Indians would be stretched to give off their best in such a competition did not manifest itself into personal bests, leave alone National records. Any talk thus of Indian athletics having benefited from this meet will be totally misplaced. So, too, any attempt to paint this meet as next only in magnitude, importance and standards to the Olympics. That will be laughable. Thin fields and empty lanes, not to speak of the absence of a large majority of the champions from either continent, projected a disappointing picture, no matter that the officials kept parroting the jingle, 'the cream of Asia v the cream of Africa.' A total of 23 Asian Games champions and 12 All-Africa Games champions, apart from eight world champions from Africa besides innumerable other medal winners from both continents were missing. And yet they kept talking about this 'cream v cream' business.

It was a wrongly timed meet and it was indeed a wonder that some of the world-class athletes such as Frankie Fredericks, Shingo Suetsugu, Tirunesh Dibaba, Meseret Defar, Silesh Sihine, Hailu Mekonnen and Gebregziabher Gebremariam competed in Hyderabad. Obviously, extra efforts were made to get at least some of them if not all. Fredericks for one praised the initiative taken by India and said that it was a "powerful concept" and in future such meets could even challenge the World championships.

The 36-year-old Namibian was the star attraction in a meet starved of big names. Despite arriving at 6 a.m. on the day of his event, the 200m, the former World champion gave a classic display, winning in an Indian all-comers' record of 20.57 seconds from Kazakh Gennadiy Chernovol and Senegalese Oumar Loum. Nigerians Deji Aliu and Uchenna Emedolu were conspicuous by their absence, but the shorter sprint title still went to a Nigerian all right. Nineteen-year-old Olufasuba Olusoji clocked a personal best of 10.15s to launch himself into top-flight international levels.

Team-mate Tamunosiki Atorudibo was second, leaving Japanese Suetsugu, the 200m bronze medallist at the Paris World championships, with the bronze. Suetsugu, like Fredericks, was a late arrival in the Andhra capital. The track events, thanks to the Ethiopians and Nigerians, generally provided a decent fare, barring the 3000m steeplechase where you had the rare sight of a Kenyan (John Kemboi) clocking 8:56.43 to win a title and another Kenyan (Joel Kiptanui Chelimo) timing 9:24.08 to be pushed to the bronze status by an Indian, Arun D'Souza. Men from the land of Kip Keino and Moses Kiptanui are not expected to clock such timings, forgetting for a moment the defeat of Chelimo to the Indian. D'Souza's 9:05.97 was well below his best of

8:50.92. Incidentally, Kemboi's timing in Hyderabad was his personal best.Talking of personal bests and all-comers' records, Olusoji's 10.15s for the 100m, Kenyan Ezra Sambu's 45.03s for the 400m, Ethiopian Hailu Mekonnen's 13:49.08 for the 5000m, Ethiopian Sileshi Sihine's 27:48.40 for the 10,000m, and Kazakh Yevgeniy Melshenko's 49.66s for the 400m hurdles were the best recorded on Indian soil. So, too, Hardus Pienaar's javelin mark of 84.50m, a personal best for the South African, and Chinese woman hammer thrower Liu Yinghui's 68.03m.

There were four National records in all. Sudanese Todd Matthews Jouda timed 13.68s to win the 110m hurdles gold in a National record time, Aissata Soulama of Burkina Faso clocked a 57.99 for the fourth place in the women's 400m hurdles, Sri Lankan Gallage Geetha Nandan timed 52:58.80 for another National mark while finishing fourth in the women's 10,000m walk and the Thai women's team timed 43.90s for the bronze in the shorter relay. Nineteen-year-old Cameroonian, Delphine Atangana had a National junior record of 23.37s while winning the women's 200m. The closest that any Indian came to a personal best was in the heptathlon where Shobha's 5884 was just four points shy of her best recorded at the same venue in the last National Games.

6

Commonwealth Games

First Commonwealth Games

The first Commonwealth Games were held in 1930 in Hamilton, Ontario, Canada. Bobby Robinson, a major influence within athletics in Canada at the time, finally implemented the event that had been talked about amongst Commonwealth nations for over thirty years. Eleven countries with 400 athletes in total participated in the first Commonwealth Games. $30,000 was provided by the City of Hamilton to these nations to help cover travelling costs. Since then, the Games have been conducted every four years except for 1942 and 1946, due to World War II. From 1930 to 1950 the Games were known as the British Empire Games, then the British Empire and Commonwealth Games until 1962. From 1966 to 1974 they took on the title of British Commonwealth Games and from 1978 onwards they have been known as simply the Commonwealth Games.

A governor-general represents her in the country. While other Games around the globe have been founded on geographic or climatic factors such as the Asian, Pan Am, African Games and Winter Olympics, the Commonwealth Games has been founded on history. Unique characteristics of the Commonwealth Games include being the only Games which shares a common language. All athletes and officials can converse with each other in English, creating an atmosphere that has led to the Commonwealth Games being long known as the "Friendly Games".

The bonds of the Commonwealth Games help to encourage and support the pursuit of health and fitness in each of the member countries and provide an inspiration for youth to strive for excellence.

The city of Hamilton proved a gracious first host of the Commonwealth Games movement and is as important to it as Athens is to the Olympics. Then called the British Empire Games, the sociological, cultural and political makeup of the Commonwealth Movement has altered substantially since 1930.

Results by Country

Country	Gold	Silver	Bronze	Total
Australia	3	4	1	8
Bermuda	-	-	-	-
Canada	20	15	19	54
England	25	23	13	61
Guyana	-	1	1	2
New Zealand	3	4	2	9
Newfoundland	-	-	-	-
Northern Ireland	-	1	-	1
Scotland	2	3	5	10
South Africa	6	4	7	17
Wales	-	2	1	3
Total Medals	59	57	49	165

The inaugural Games was utilitarian and very down to earth, proving that more doesn't necessarily mean better.

The athletes' village was the Prince of Wales School next to the Civic Stadium, where the competitors slept two dozen to a classroom. Despite missing some basic comforts, the participants were unanimous in their praise for the Games and Hamilton's hospitality. Eleven countries sent a total of about 400 athletes to the Hamilton Games.

Women competed in only the swimming events. The participant nations were Australia, Bermuda, British Guiana, Canada, England, Northern Ireland, Newfoundland, New Zealand, Scotland, South Africa and Wales. The Hamilton Games featured six sports: track and field, boxing, lawn bowls, rowing, swimming and diving, and wrestling and ran at a cost of $97,973.00.

1934 British Empire Games

Sixteen nations sent a total of about 500 competitors to the London Games. In addition to the 11 nations that had competed at the 1930 Hamilton Games, making their debut at the London Games were Hong Kong, India, Jamaica, Zimbabwe (Rhodesia) and Trinidad. This was also to be the last time that Newfoundland took independent of Canada.

Six sports were featured in the Games - athletics, boxing, cycling, lawn bowls, swimming and diving, and wrestling. A highlight of the 1934 Games was the inclusion of events for women in athletics, with careful consideration given not to include events that were considered 'too exhaustive'. The running events were restricted to the short sprints and a shortened 4 x 220 yard relay instead of the 4 x 440 yard realy as per the men's program. Nevertheless this was a breakthrough for women in sport that would one day lead to full recognition and programming for women's athletics on the international stage.

The athletes oath was read by the captain for the England Athletics team, R.L. Howland as follows:

"We declare that we are loyal subjects of His Majesty the King, Emporer, and will take part in the British Empire Games in the spirit of true sportsmanship, recognising the rules which govern them and desirous of participating in them for the honour of our Empire and the Glory of Sport."

Originally scheduled for Johannesburg, South Africa, the II Games were hosted by London, in order to avoid a political crisis over South Africa's 'Apartheid' policy and its implications on visiting Commonwealth athletes and officials.

Results by Country

Country	Gold	Silver	Bronze	Total
Australia	8	4	2	14
Bermuda	-	-	-	-
Canada	17	25	9	51
England	29	20	24	73
Guyana	1	-	-	1
India	-	-	1	1
Jamaica	-	1	1	2
New Zealand	1	-	2	3
Newfoundland	-	-	-	-
Northern Ireland	-	1	2	3
Scotland	5	4	17	26
South Africa	7	10	5	22
Trinidad & Tobago	-	-	-	-
Wales	-	3	3	6
Zimbabwe	-	-	2	2
Total Medals	68	68	68	204

1938 British Empire Games

Held in the southern hemisphere for the first time, the III Games opening ceremony took place at the famed Sydney Cricket Ground in front of 40,000 spectators who were keen to see Australia and New Zealand excel against England in particular.

Fifteen nations participated down under at the Sydney Games involving a total of 466 athletes and 43 officials. New participants included Fiji and Ceylon.

Seven sports were featured in the Sydney Games - track and field, boxing, cycling, lawn bowls, rowing, swimming and diving, and wrestling.

Results by Country

Country	Gold	Silver	Bronze	Total
Australia	25	19	22	66
Bermuda	-	-	-	-
Canada	13	16	15	44
England	15	15	10	40
Fiji	-	-	-	-
Guyana	-	1	-	1
India	-	-	-	-
New Zealand	5	7	13	25
Northern Ireland	-	-	-	-
Scotland	-	2	3	5
South Africa	10	10	6	26
Sri Lanka	1	-	-	1
Trinidad & Tobago	-	-	-	-
Wales	2	1	-	3
Zimbabwe	-	-	2	2
Total Medals	71	71	71	213

1950 British Empire Games

World War II interrupted the staging of the British Empire Games scheduled for 1942 and 1946, however the enthusiasm from within the British Empire to continue what was started in 1930 was still strong enough for interest to be shown in their revival.

Awarded to New Zealand, the IV Games were held at the nation's largest city, Auckland. New Zealand had never been the focus of so much sporting attention and the hosts responded in a most magnificent and hospitable manner.

The opening ceremony at Eden Park was attended by 40,000 spectators, whilst nearly 250,000 people attended the Auckland Games, paying out a total of £89,435 as event spectators.

Results by Country

Country	Gold	Silver	Bronze	Total
Australia	34	27	19	80
Canada	8	9	13	30
England	19	16	13	48
Fiji	1	2	2	5
Malaya	2	1	1	4
New Zealand	10	22	22	54
Nigeria	-	1	-	1
Scotland	5	3	2	10
South Africa	8	4	8	20
Sri Lanka	1	2	-	3
Wales	-	1	-	1
Zimbabwe	-	1	-	1
Total Medals	88	89	80	257

The atmosphere of the Opening Ceremony is best described by this paragraph from the Official Record of the Games:

> "The entrance of the gladiators in the days of ancient Athens and ancient Rome could not have been more impressive than was that Parade at Eden Park on the afternoon of February 4, 1950. As one, the crowd stitted by the majesty of the colourful scene, wonderful too in its simplicity, rose to its feet to remain standing throughout the ceremony, cheering to the echo as the parade passed on its way around the stadium..."

Twelve countries sent a total of 495 male and 95 female competitors to Auckland. Newly formed Malaysia and Nigeria made their first appearance. Nine sports featured at the Auckland Games - track and field, boxing, cycling, fencing, lawn bowls, rowing, swimming and diving, weightlifting and wrestling.

1954 British Empire & Commonwealth Games

The awarding of the Games to Vancouver, was the culmination of two years of very hard work by an enterprising group of Civic leaders spearheaded by then Mayor, Charles E. Thompson. Vancouver then proceeded to set new standards in organisation and presentation of not only Commonwealth Games but all multi-sport Games of the times.

The athletes oath was taken by the captain of the Canadian team, Mr Bill Parnell, which for the first time would reflect the involvement of Commonwealth nations, outside of the British Empire.

The Fifth (V) Games, placed Vancouver on a world stage and featured memorable sporting moments as well as outstanding entertainment, technical innovation and cultural events. The 'Miracle Mile', as it became dubbed, saw both the gold medallist, Roger Bannister of England, and silver medallist, John Landy of Australia, run sub-four minute races in an event that was televised live across the globe for the first time.

Results by Country

Country	Gold	Silver	Bronze	Total
Australia	21	11	17	49
Bahamas	-	-	-	-
Barbados	-	1	-	1
Bermuda	-	-	-	-
Canada	9	21	14	44
England	23	24	20	67
Fiji	-	-	-	-
Ghana	-	-	-	-
Guyana	-	-	1	1
Hong Kong	-	1	-	1
India	-	-	-	-
Jamaica	1	-	-	1
Kenya	-	-	-	-
New Zealand	7	7	5	19
Nigeria	1	3	3	7
Northern Ireland	2	1	-	3
Pakistan	1	3	2	6
Scotland	6	2	5	13
South Africa	16	6	14	36
Trinidad & Tobago	2	2	-	4
Uganda	-	1	-	1
Wales	1	1	5	7
Zambia	-	-	1	1
Zimbabwe	3	6	3	12
Total Medals	93	90	90	273

Some 24 nations sent a total of 662 athletes and 127 officials to the Vancouver Games. This was a 'qantum leap' in size for the Commonwealth Games and represented the most significant increase in (100%) for any Commonwealth Games.

Nations winning medals at the Games included England, Australia, South Africa, Canada, New Zealand, Scotland, Trinidad, Northern Ireland, (Zimbabwe)North and South Rhodesia, Nigeria, Pakistan, Wales, Jamaica, Hong Kong, Uganda, Barbados and British Guiana.

1958 British Empire & Commonwealth Games

The VI Games marked the largest sporting event ever held in Wales and it was the smallest Country ever to host a British Empire and Commonwealth Games. Cardiff had to wait 12 years longer than originally scheduled to become host of the Games, as the 1946 event was cancelled because of World War II.

"The triumph of Wales and Cardiff in staging the Sixth British Empire and Commonwealth Games is now history - and history that will ring down the years to come".

England's famed middle distance runners, Roger Bannister and Chris Chattaway, were handed the honour of taking the Queen's Baton from Buckingham Palace on the first stage of its journey to Wales.

The Cardiff Games were to be South Africa's last until their post-apartheid return to the Games in 1994. A number of objections against South Africa took place in Cardiff because their team had been selected on the basis of race and colour rather than ability. South Africa subsequently withdrew from the Commonwealth in 1961 for 30 years.

Thirty-five nations sent a total of 1,130 athletes and 228 officials to the Cardiff Games and 23 countries and dependencies won medals, including, for the first time, Singapore, Ghana, Kenya and the Isle of Man.

Nine sports were featured in the Cardiff Games – athletics, boxing, cycling, fencing, lawn bowls, rowing, swimming and diving, weightlifting and wrestling.

Results by Country

Country	Gold	Silver	Bronze	Total
Australia	27	22	17	66
Bahamas	1	1	-	2
Barbados	1	1	-	2
Canada	1	10	16	27
Dominica	-	-	-	-
England	29	22	29	80
Fiji	-	-	-	-
Ghana	-	-	1	1
Gilbraltar	-	-	-	-
Guyana	-	1	-	1
Hong Kong	-	-	-	-
India	2	1	-	3
Isle of Man	-	-	1	1
Jamaica	4	2	1	7
Jersey	-	-	-	-
Kenya	-	-	2	2
Malaya	-	2	-	2
Malta	-	-	-	-
Mauritius	-	-	-	-
New Zealand	4	6	9	19
Nigeria	-	1	1	2
Northern Ireland	1	1	3	5
Pakistan	3	5	2	10
Sabah	-	-	-	-
Sarawak	-	-	-	-
Scotland	5	5	3	13
Sierra Leone	-	-	-	-
Singapore	2	-	-	2
South Africa	13	10	8	31
Sri Lanka	-	-	-	-
St. Vincent & Grenadines	-	-	-	-
Trinidad & Tobago	-	-	1	1
Uganda	-	1	-	1
Wales	1	3	7	11
Zimbabwe	-	-	3	3
Total Medals	94	94	104	292

1962 British Empire & Commonwealth Games

The VII Commonwealth Games are remembered for its "heat, dust and glory". The day before the Perth Games opened the temperature was an expected 80 degrees Fahrenheit, but the heat was measured at 105 degrees at the opening ceremony in the new Perry Lakes Stadium the following day and such extremes persisted throughout the Games' duration. In the previous 65 years, only 10 100 degree plus days had been recorded in Perth. Australian soldiers were pressed into action, ferrying water to competing athletes.

James Coote of the London Daily Telegraph describes:

> "The VIIth Commonwealth Games have proved that it is possible for an area as basically devoid of sports interest as Perth to stage the second most important sports meeting in the World - and stage it successfully. Perth has shown that these Games will continue for years to come"

Thirty-five countries sent a total of 1,041 athletes and officials to Perth. Jersey was amongst the medal winners for the first time, whilst British Honduras, Dominica, Papua New Guinea and St Lucia all made their inaugural Games appearances. Aden also competed by special invitation. Sabah, Sarawak and Malaya competed for the last time before taking part in 1966 under the Malaysian flag. Nine sports were featured at the Perth Games - athletics, boxing, cycling, fencing, lawn bowls, rowing, swimming and diving, weightlifting and wrestling.

For Perth, the staging of the Commonwealth Games provided it with a springboard for phenominal development in sport and recreation, centered around the sports facilities that were built for the Games. These facilities have catered not only for elite sport but provided much needed opportunity for the development of organised recreational sport as well as a focus for Australia's first University degree Program in Physical Education.

Results by Country

Country	Gold	Silver	Bronze	Total
Aden	-	-	-	-
Australia	38	36	31	105
Bahamas	-	1	-	1
Barbados	-	-	1	1
Belize	-	-	-	-
Canada	4	12	15	31
Dominica	-	-	-	-
England	29	22	27	78
Fiji	-	-	2	2
Ghana	3	5	1	9
Gilbraltar	-	-	-	-
Guyana	-	-	1	1
Hong Kong	-	-	-	-
Isle of Man	-	-	-	-
Jamaica	3	1	1	5
Jersey	-	-	1	1
Kenya	2	2	1	5
Malaya	-	-	1	1
Malta	-	-	-	-
Mauritius	-	-	-	-
New Zealand	10	12	10	32
Northern Ireland	-	-	1	1
Pakistan	8	1	-	9
Papua New Guinea	-	-	1	1
Sabah	-	-	-	-
Sarawak	-	-	-	-
Scotland	4	7	3	14
Singapore	2	-	-	2
Sri Lanka	-	-	-	-
St. Lucia	-	-	-	-
Tanzania	-	-	-	-
Trinidad & Tobago	-	-	2	2
Uganda	1	1	4	6
Wales	-	2	4	6
Zimbabwe	-	2	5	7
Total Medals	104	104	112	320

1966 British Empire & Commonwealth Games

With the British Empire formally ended, the Kingston Games became the VIII British Commonwealth Games. There was a worry amongst the larger nations that Jamaica's infrastructure would not enable a successful Games delivery - but this proved to be largely unfounded. Controversially, also, the event programme was altered for the first time since 1950 with lawn bowls and rowing dropped and replaced with badminton and shooting instead.

Thirty-four nations (including Aden and Saudi Arabia) competed in the Kingston Games sending a total of 1,316 athletes and officials.

The nine sports featured in the Kingston Games were athletics, badminton, boxing, cycling, fencing, shooting, swimming and diving, weightlifting and wrestling.

Results by Country

Country	Gold	Silver	Bronze	Total
Aden	-	-	-	-
Antigua & Barbuda	-	-	-	-
Australia	23	28	22	73
Bahamas	-	1	-	1
Barbados	-	-	1	1
Belize	-	-	-	-
Bermuda	-	1	-	1
Canada	14	20	23	57
England	33	24	23	80
Fiji	-	-	-	-
Ghana	5	2	2	9
Gilbraltar	-	-	-	-
Guyana	-	1	-	1

(Contd...)

India	3	4	3	10
Isle of Man	1	-	-	1
Jamaica	-	4	8	12
Jersey	-	-	-	-
Kenya	4	1	3	8
Malaysia	2	2	1	5
Mauritius	-	-	-	-
New Zealand	8	5	13	26
Nigeria	3	4	3	10
Northern Ireland	1	3	3	7
Pakistan	4	1	4	9
Papua New Guinea	-	1	-	1
Saudi Arabia	-	-	-	-
Scotland	1	4	4	9
Sierra Leone	-	-	-	-
Singapore	-	-	-	-
Sri Lanka	-	-	-	-
St. Vincent & Grenadines	-	-	-	-
Tanzania	-	-	-	-
Trinidad & Tobago	5	2	2	9
Uganda	-	-	3	3
Wales	3	2	2	7
Total Medals	110	110	120	340

1970 British Commonwealth Games

The IX Games from the 16th to the 25th of July, 1970 in Edinburgh will be remembered for a number of firsts. It was the first time that metric distances and electronic photo-finish technology were employed at the Games and also the first time that HM Queen Elizabeth II attended in her capacity as Head of the Commonwealth. Scots will further remember the Games for the Stewart brothers Ian (gold) and Peter (4th) in the 5000 metres and

Lachie Stewart (no relation) who took gold in the 10000 metres.

Forty-two nations sent a total of nearly 1,750 athletes and officials to the first Edinburgh Games. New medal winning nations included Tanzania, Malawi and St Vincent.

Ten sports were featured in the Games - athletics, badminton, boxing, cycling, fencing, lawn bowls, shooting, swimming and diving, weightlifting and wrestling.

Results by Country

Country	Gold	Silver	Bronze	Total
Antigua & Barbuda	-	-	-	-
Australia	36	24	22	82
Bahamas	-	-	-	-
Barbados	-	1	-	1
Bermuda	-	-	-	-
Canada	18	24	24	66
Dominica	-	-	-	-
England	27	25	32	84
Fiji	-	-	1	1
Ghana	2	3	2	7
Gilbraltar	-	-	-	-
Grenada	-	-	-	-
Guernsey	-	-	-	-
Guyana	-	-	1	1
Hong Kong	1	-	-	1
India	5	3	4	12
Isle of Man	-	-	1	1
Jamaica	4	2	1	7

(Contd...)

Jersey	-	-	-	-
Kenya	5	3	6	14
Malawi	-	-	1	1
Malaysia	1	1	1	3
Malta	-	-	-	-
Mauritius	-	-	-	-
New Zealand	2	6	6	14
Nigeria	2	-	-	2
Northern Ireland	3	1	5	9
Pakistan	4	3	3	10
Papua New Guinea	-	-	-	-
Scotland	6	8	11	25
Sierra Leone	-	-	-	-
Singapore	-	1	1	2
Sri Lanka	-	-	-	-
St. Lucia	-	-	-	-
St. Vincent & Grenadines	-	-	1	1
Swaziland	-	-	-	-
Tanzania	-	1	-	1
The Gambia	-	-	1	1
Trinidad & Tobago	-	4	3	7
Uganda	3	3	1	7
Wales	2	6	4	12
Zambia	-	2	2	4
Total Medals	121	121	134	376

1974 British Commonwealth Games

Following the massacre of Israeli athletes at the 1972 Munich Olympics, the X Games at Christchurch was the first multi-sport event to place the safety of participants and spectators as its uppermost requirement. Security guards surrounded the athlete's village and there was an exceptionally high-profile police presence. Even so, Christchurch enchanted the watching world as a city of beautiful churches and gardens.

On the running track, Jamaica's Don Quarrie successfully defended both his 1970 100m and 200m gold medals. Quarrie was to go on to win the 1978 100m as well.

Only 22 countries succeeded in winning medals from the total haul of 374 medals on offer, but first time winners included Western Samoa, Lesotho and Swaziland.

Nine sports were featured in the Christchurch Games - athletics, badminton, boxing, cycling, lawn bowls, shooting, swimming and diving, weightlifting and wrestling.

Results by Country

Country	Gold	Silver	Bronze	Total
Australia	29	28	25	82
Barbados	-	-	-	-
Bermuda	-	-	-	-
Botswana	-	-	-	-
Canada	25	19	18	62
Cook Islands	-	-	-	-
England	28	31	21	80
Fiji	-	-	-	-
Ghana	1	3	5	9
Gilbraltar	-	-	-	-
Grenada	-	-	-	-
Guernsey	-	-	-	-
Hong Kong	-	-	-	-
India	4	8	3	15

(Contd...)

Isle of Man	-	-	-	-
Jamaica	2	1	-	3
Jersey	-	-	-	-
Kenya	7	2	9	18
Lesotho	-	-	-	-
Malawi	-	-	-	-
Malaysia	1	-	3	4
Mauritius	-	-	-	-
New Zealand	9	8	18	35
Nigeria	3	3	4	10
Northern Ireland	3	1	2	6
Papua New Guinea	-	-	-	-
Samoa	-	1	1	2
Scotland	3	5	11	19
Singapore	-	-	1	1
St.Vincent & Grenadines	1	-	-	1
Swaziland	-	-	1	1
Tanzania	1	-	1	2
The Gambia	-	-	-	-
Tonga	-	-	-	-
Trinidad&Tobago	-	1	1	2
Uganda	2	4	3	9
Wales	1	5	4	10
Zambia	1	1	1	3
Total Medals	121	121	132	374

1978 British Commonwealth Games

The XI Games was the first to bear the current day name of the Commonwealth Games. Whilst Edmonton had won the right to host the Games with an audacious vision presented six years earlier to the Commonwealth Games Federation General Assembly, the organisers had to walk a careful tightrope in the immediate run up to the Edmonton Games to ensure that there was no repeat of the African nations boycott of the 1976 Montreal Olympics caused by a New Zealand rugby tour of South Africa.

Forty-six countries sent a total of 1,405 athletes and 504 officials to the Edmonton Games. As host nation, Canada also topped the medal table for the first time.

Ten sports were featured at the Edmonton Games - athletics, badminton, boxing, cycling, gymnastics, lawn bowls, shooting, swimming and diving, weightlifting and wrestling.

Results by Country

Country	Gold	Silver	Bronze	Total
Antigua & Barbuda	-	-	-	-
Australia	24	33	27	84
Bahamas	-	1	-	1
Bangladesh	-	-	-	-
Barbados	-	-	-	-
Belize	-	-	-	-
Bermuda	-	-	-	-
Canada	45	31	33	109
Cayman Islands	-	-	-	-
Cyprus	-	-	-	-
England	27	28	32	87
Fiji	-	-	-	-
Ghana	1	1	1	3
Gilbraltar	-	-	-	-
Grenada	-	-	-	-
Guernsey	-	-	-	-
Guyana	1	1	1	3

(Contd...)

Hong Kong	2	-	-	2
India	5	4	6	15
Isle of Man	-	-	1	1
Jamaica	2	2	3	7
Jersey	-	-	-	-
Kenya	7	6	5	18
Lesotho	-	-	-	-
Malawi	-	-	-	-
Malaysia	1	2	1	4
Mauritius	-	-	-	-
New Zealand	5	6	9	20
Northern Ireland	2	1	2	5
Papua New Guinea	-	1	-	1
Samoa	-	-	3	3
Scotland	3	6	5	14
Sierra Leone	-	-	-	-
Singapore	-	-	-	-
Sri Lanka	-	-	-	-
St. Kitts	-	-	-	-
St. Lucia	-	-	-	-
St. Vincent & Grenadines	-	-	-	-
Swaziland	-	-	-	-
Tanzania	1	1	-	2
The Gambia	-	-	-	-
Trinidad & Tobago	-	2	2	4
Turks & Caicos Islands	-	-	-	-
Wales	2	1	5	8
Zambia	-	2	2	4
Zimbabwe	-	-	-	-
Total Medals	128	129	138	395

1982 Commonwealth Games

The Brisbane Games are still hailed as one of the very best. Everything went so well from the moment Matilda, a 13-metre mechanical kangaroo, helped out with the opening ceremonies. Once again, a boycott was avoided and the sun shone throughout the duration of the XII Games.

Forty-six nations participated in the Brisbane Games with a new record total of 1,583 athletes and 571 officials. As hosts, Australia headed the medal table leading the way ahead of England, Canada, Scotland and New Zealand respectively.

The men's 200m gold was shared by England's Mike McFarlane and Scotland's Allan Wells, with judges unable to separate the pair at the winning post.

Nine sports featured at the Brisbane Games – athletics, badminton, boxing, cycling, lawn bowls, shooting, swimming and diving, weightlifting and wrestling.

Results by Country

Country	Gold	Silver	Bronze	Total
Australia	39	39	29	107
Bahamas	2	2	2	6
Barbados	-	-	-	-
Bermuda	-	-	1	1
Botswana	-	-	-	-
Canada	26	23	33	82
Cayman Islands	-	-	-	-
Cyprus	-	-	-	-
England	38	38	32	108
Fiji	1	-	-	1

(Contd...)

Ghana	-	-	-	-
Gilbraltar	-	-	-	-
Guernsey	-	1	1	2
Guyana	-	-	-	-
Hong Kong	1	-	-	1
India	5	8	3	16
Isle of Man	-	-	-	-
Jamaica	2	1	1	4
Kenya	4	2	4	10
Malawi	-	-	-	-
Malaysia	1	-	1	2
Malta	-	-	-	-
Mauritius	-		-	-
New Zealand	5	8	13	26
Nigeria	[illegible]	-	8	13
Northern Ireland	-	3	3	6
Papua New Guinea	-	-	-	-
Samoa	-	-	-	-
Scotland	8	6	12	26
Singapore	-	-	1	1
Solomon Islands	-	-	-	-
St. Helena	-	-	-	-
Swaziland	-	-	1	1
Tanzania	1	2	2	5
The Gambia	-	-	-	-
Tonga	-	-	-	-
Trinidad & Tobago	-	-	-	-
Uganda	-	3	-	3
Vanuatu	-	-	-	-
Wales	4	4	1	9
Zambia	-	1	5	6
Zimbabwe	1	-	-	1
Total Medals	143	141	153	437

1986 COMMONWEALTH GAMES

After nearly two decades successfully averting political stay-aways and protests because of apartheid and sanction-busting sports tours to South Africa, the XIII Games, the second to be staged at Edinburgh, was to become known as "the Boycott Games". Sadly, despite there being so many fond memories of the Scottish hospitality offered in 1970, 32 Commonwealth nations decided that they could not attend, because of their opposition to apartheid in sports.

Twenty-six nations did attend the second Edinburgh Games and sent a total of 1,662 athletes and 461 officials. Ten sports were featured at the second Edinburgh Games - athletics, aquatics, badminton, boxing, cycling, lawn bowls, rowing, shooting, weightlifting and wrestling.

Results by Country

Country	Gold	Silver	Bronze	Total
Australia	40	46	35	121
Botswana	-	-	1	1
Canada	51	35	31	117
Cook Islands	-	-	-	-
England	52	43	49	144
Fiji	-	-	-	-
Gilbraltar	-	-	-	-
Guernsey	-	2	-	2
Hong Kong	-	1	2	3
Isle of Man	1	-	-	1
Jersey	-	-	1	1
Lesotho	-	-	-	-
Malawi	-	-	2	2

(Contd...)

New Zealand	8	16	14	38
Northern Ireland	2	4	9	15
Scotland	3	12	18	33
Singapore	-	-	1	1
Swaziland	-	1	-	1
Vanuatu	-	-	-	-
Wales	6	5	11	22
Total Medals	163	165	174	502

1990 Commonwealth Games

The XIV Commonwealth Games, the third to be hosted by New Zealand and Auckland's second, witnessed a fantastic opening ceremony comprising a magnificent and moving portrayal of the forces that led to the formation of New Zealand society and culture.

Thankfully, the perennially threatened boycott gave way to a new positive spirit of co-operation far more in keeping with the image of "The Friendly Games" and a new record of 54 nations participated in the second Auckland Games.

Twenty-nine of the competing nations succeeded in winning medals from a total of 639 medals available. Australia headed the medals table with New Zealand claiming fourth place behind England and Canada.

Ten sports featured in the second Auckland Games – athletics, aquatics, badminton, boxing, cycling, gymnastics, judo, lawn bowls, shooting and weightlifting.

Results by Country

Country	Gold	Silver	Bronze	Total
Australia	52	54	55	161
Bahamas	-	-	2	2

(Contd...)

Bangladesh	1	-	1	2
Barbados	-	-	-	-
Bermuda	1	-	-	1
Botswana	-	-	-	-
British Virgin Islands	-	-	-	-
Brunei Darussalam	-	-	-	-
Canada	36	42	37	115
Cayman Islands	-	-	-	-
Cook Islands	-	-	-	-
Cyprus	1	1	-	2
England	47	40	42	129
Falkland Islands	-	-	-	-
Ghana	-	2	-	2
Guernsey	1	-	-	1
Guyana	-	-	1	1
Hong Kong	1	1	3	5
India	13	8	11	32
Isle of Man	-	-	-	-
Jamaica	2	-	2	4
Jersey	1	-	1	2
Kenya	6	9	3	18
Lesotho	-	-	-	-
Malawi	-	-	-	-
Malaysia	2	2	-	4
Maldives	-	-	-	-
Malta	-	-	1	1
Mauritius	-	-	-	-
Nauru	1	2	-	3
New Zealand	17	14	27	58
Nigeria	5	13	7	25
Norfolk Island	-	-	-	-
Northern Ireland	1	3	5	9
Pakistan	-	-	-	-

(Contd...)

Papua New Guinea	1	-	-	1
Samoa	-	-	2	2
Scotland	5	7	10	22
Seychelles	-	-	-	-
Sierra Leone	-	-	-	-
Solomon Islands	-	-	-	-
Sri Lanka	-	-	-	-
St. Kitts	-	-	-	-
Swaziland	-	-	-	-
Tanzania	-	1	2	3
The Gambia	-	-	-	-
Tonga	-	-	-	-
Trinidad & Tobago	-	-	-	-
Uganda	2	-	2	4
Vanuatu	-	-	-	-
Wales	10	3	12	25
Zambia	-	-	3	3
Zimbabwe	-	2	1	3
Total Medals	206	204	230	640

1994 Commonwealth Games

Following the successful Victoria delegation to the Commonwealth Games Federation in 1988, the XV Games were held in Canada for the fourth time. The end of apartheid in the early part of the decade also heralded the return of South Africa to the Commonwealth Games and ensured that the era of threatened boycotts was over. Both the opening and closing ceremonies were held at Victoria's Centennial Stadium, which had undergone a superb refit in honour of the Games.

Sixty-three nations sent a total of nearly 2,450 athletes and 892 officials as the Commonwealth Games burgeoned at Victoria. Once again, Australia headed the medals table whilst the hosts, Canada, pushed England into third place. Nigeria marked its arrival as a Commonwealth sporting force by picking up more gold medals than both New Zealand and India. Hong Kong said farewell to the Games with the territory becoming a special administrative region of the People's Republic of China in 1997.

Ten sports were featured at the Victoria Games - athletics, aquatics, badminton, boxing, cycling, gymnastics, lawn bowls, shooting, weightlifting and wrestling.

Results by Country

Country	Gold	Silver	Bronze	Total
Antigua & Barbuda	-	-	-	-
Australia	87	52	43	182
Bahamas	-	-	-	-
Bangladesh	-	-	-	-
Barbados	-	-	-	-
Belize	-	-	-	-
Bermuda	-	-	1	1
Botswana	-	-	1	1
British Virgin Islands	-	-	-	-
Brunei Darussalam	-	-	-	-
Canada	40	42	46	128
Cyprus	2	1	2	5
Dominica	-	-	-	-
England	31	45	49	125
Falkland Islands	-	-	-	-
Ghana	-	-	1	1
Guernsey	-	-	1	1
Guyana	-	-	-	-
Hong Kong	-	-	4	4
India	6	11	7	24
Isle of Man	-	-	-	-
Jamaica	2	4	2	8

(Contd...)

Jersey	-	-	-	-
Kenya	7	4	8	19
Lesotho	-	-	-	-
Malawi	-	-	-	-
Malaysia	2	3	2	7
Maldives	-	-	-	-
Malta	-	-	-	-
Mauritius	-	-	-	-
Montserrat	-	-	-	-
Namibia	1	-	1	2
Nauru	3	-	-	3
NewZealand	5	16	20	41
Nigeria	11	13	13	37
Norfolk Island	-	-	1	1
Northern Ireland	5	2	3	10
Pakistan	-	-	3	3
Papua New Guinea	-	1	-	1
Samoa	-	1	-	1
Scotland	6	3	11	20
Seychelles	-	-	1	1
Sierra Leone	-	-	-	-
Singapore	-	-	-	-
South Africa	2	4	5	11
Sri Lanka	1	2	-	3
St. Kitts	-	-	-	-
St. Lucia	-	-	-	-
St. Vincent& Grenadines	-	-	-	-
Swaziland	-	-	-	-
Tanzania	-	-	1	1
The Gambia	-	-	-	-
Tonga	-	-	1	1
Trinidad&Tobago	-	-	2	2
Uganda	-	-	2	2
Vanuatu	-	-	-	-
Wales	5	8	6	19
Zambia	1	1	2	4
Zimbabwe	-	3	3	6
Total Medals	217	216	242	675

1998 Commonwealth Games

For the first time in its 68-year history, the Commonwealth Games were held in Asia. The XVI Games, held in Kuala Lumpur were also the first Games to feature team sports - an overwhelming success that added large numbers to both participators and TV audience numbers.

A new record of 70 countries sent a total of 5,250 athletes and officials to the Kuala Lumpur Games. The top five countries in the medal standing were Australia, England, Canada, Malaysia and South Africa. Nauru also achieved an impressive haul of three gold medals.

Fifteen sports were featured in the Kuala Lumpur Games - aquatics, athletics, badminton, boxing, cricket, cycling, gymnastics, hockey, netball, lawn bowls, rugby 7s, shooting, tenpin bowling, weightlifting and wrestling.

Results by Country

Country	Gold	Silver	Bronze	Total
Anguilla	-	-	-	-
Antigua & Barbuda	-	-	-	-
Australia	80	61	57	198
Bahamas	1	1	-	2
Barbados	1	-	2	3
Belize	-	-	-	-
Bermuda	-	1	-	1
Botswana	-	-	-	-
British Virgin Islands	-	-	-	-
Cameroon	-	3	3	6
Canada	30	31	38	99
Cook Islands	-	-	-	-

(Contd...)

Cyprus	1	1	1	3
Dominica	-	-	-	-
England	36	47	53	136
Falkland Islands	-	-	-	-
Fiji	-	1	-	1
Ghana	1	1	3	5
Grenada	-	-	-	-
India	7	10	8	25
Isle of Man	-	1	-	1
Jamaica	4	2	-	6
Kenya	7	5	4	16
Lesotho	1	-	-	1
Malawi	-	-	-	-
Malaysia	10	14	12	36
Maldives	-	-	-	-
Malta	-	-	-	-
Mauritius	1	1	2	4
Montserrat	-	-	-	-
Mozambique	1	1	-	2
Namibia	-	2	1	3
Nauru	3	-	-	3
New Zealand	8	6	20	34
Norfolk Island	-	-	-	-
Northern Ireland	2	1	2	5
Pakistan	-	1	-	1
Papua New Guinea	-	-	1	1
Samoa	-	-	-	-
Scotland	3	2	7	12
Seychelles	-	2	-	2
Sierra Leone	-	-	-	-
Singapore	-	-	-	-

(Contd...)

Solomon Islands	-	-	-	-
South Africa	9	11	14	34
Sri Lanka	-	1	1	2
St. Kitts	-	-	-	-
St. Lucia	-	-	-	-
St. Vincent & The Grenadines	-	-	-	-
Swaziland	-	-	-	-
Tanzania	1	1	1	3
The Gambia	-	-	-	-
Tonga	-	-	-	-
Trinidad & Tobago	1	1	1	3
Turks & Caicos Islands	-	-	-	-
Uganda	-	-	1	1
Vanuatu	-	-	-	-
Wales	3	4	8	15
Zambia	-	-	1	1
Zimbabwe	2	-	3	5
Total Medals	213	213	244	670

2002 Commonwealth Games

The city of Manchester is the capital of the North West and is the commercial, educational and cultural focus for this vibrant region of England. As well as having a population of over 400,000, 60 per cent of the population of Britain, more than 33 million people, live within a two hour drive of Manchester. Manchester is an international destination for conferences and exhibitions with more than 200,000 bed spaces within one hour's drive of the city centre.

The XVII Commonwealth Games was a world-class event and the most significant multi-sport event to be held in Great Britain since the Olympics of 1948. It was the largest in the history of the Commonwealth Games with participating athletes from 72 nations competing in 14 individual sports and three team sports from 25 July - 4 August 2002.

The sports contested were:Aquatics, Athletics, Badminton, Boxing, Cycling, Gymnastics, Hockey, Judo, Lawn Bowls, Netball, Rugby 7s, Shooting, Squash, Table Tennis, Triathlon, Weightlifting and Wrestling.

Results by Country

Country	Gold	Silver	Bronze	Total
Anguilla	-	-	-	-
Antigua & Barbuda	-	-	-	-
Australia	82	62	63	207
Bahamas	4	-	4	8
Bangladesh	1	-	-	1
Barbados	-	-	1	1
Belize	-	-	-	-
Bermuda	-	-	-	-
Botswana	-	2	1	3
British Virgin Islands	-	-	-	-
Cameroon	9	1	2	12
Canada	31	41	44	116
Cayman Islands	-	-	1	1
Cook Islands	-	-	-	-
Cyprus	2	1	1	4
Dominica	-	-	-	-
England	54	51	60	165
Fiji	1	1	1	3
Ghana	-	-	1	1
Gilbraltar	-	-	-	-
Grenada	-	-	-	-

(Contd...)

Guernsey	-	-	-	-
Guyana	1	-	-	1
India	30	22	17	69
Isle of Man	-	-	-	-
Jamaica	4	6	7	17
Jersey	-	-	-	-
Kenya	4	8	4	16
Kiribati	-	-	-	-
Lesotho	-	-	1	1
Malawi	-	-	-	-
Malaysia	7	9	18	34
Maldives	-	-	-	-
Malta	-	-	1	1
Mauritius	-	-	1	1
Montserrat	-	-	-	-
Mozambique	1	-	-	1
Namibia	1	-	4	5
Nauru	2	5	8	15
New Zealand	11	13	21	45
Nigeria	5	3	11	19
Niue	-	-	-	-
Norfolk Island	-	-	-	-
Northern Ireland	2	2	1	5
Pakistan	1	3	4	8
Papua New Guinea	-	-	-	-
Samoa	-	1	2	3
Scotland	6	8	16	30
Seychelles	-	-	-	-
Sierra Leone	-	-	-	-
Singapore	4	2	7	13
Solomon Islands	-	-	-	-

(Contd...)

South Africa	9	20	17	46
Sri Lanka	-	-	-	-
St. Kitts	1	-	-	1
St. Lucia	-	-	1	1
St. Vincent & Grenadines	-	-	-	-
Swaziland	-	-	-	-
Tanzania	1	-	1	2
The Gambia	-	-	-	-
Tonga	-	-	-	-
Trinidad & Tobago	-	1	-	1
Turks & Caicos Islands	-	-	-	-
Uganda	-	2	-	2
Vanuatu	-	-	-	-
ales	6	13	12	31
Zambia	1	1	1	3
Zimbabwe	1	1	-	2
Total Medals	282	279	334	895

2006 COMMONWEALTH GAMES

The Australian city of Melbourne, will host the Commonwealth Games in 2006. Melbourne was the location for the 1956 Olympic Games, and 50 years on will host a Commonwealth Games.

Melbourne is the capital of the State of Victoria and the second largest city in Australia with a population of nearly 3,500,000 people. The city is a multicultural one, known for its arts, culture, parks and gardens, restaurants and sport.

The Melbourne Games will have one village which will house both the athletes and team officials, located within three kilometres of the city centre. The majority of the sports venues are located along the Yarra River within the city precinct and are of world class standard.

The Opening Ceremony and Athletics competition will be held at the Melbourne Cricket Ground, one of the world's largest and most outstanding outdoor sporting grounds. It seats approximately 100,000 spectators.

The Sports that will be contested are: Aquatics, Athletics, Badminton, Basketball, Bowls, Boxing, Cycling, Gymnastics, Hockey, Netball, Rugby 7s, Shooting, Squash, Table Tennis, Triathlon and Weightlifting.To get the latest on preparations for the Games follow the link opposite to the official Games website for Melbourne 2006.

2010 Commonwealth Games

The city of New Delhi, home to 13.8 million people, will host the Commonwealth Games in 2010. This will be the first time India has hosted the Games and only the second time the event has been held in Asia.

Delhi is the capital city of India and is rich in culture and history. It stands on the western end of the Gangetic Plain and is bordered by the states of Uttar Pradesh and Haryana. There are two main districts of the city, Old Delhi the capital of Muslim India between the mid 17th and late 19th centuries with its historic sites, mosques and monuments and New Delhi, the imperial city created by the British Raj with its imposing government buildings and tree lined avenues.

The proposed dates for the Games are Saturday 23 October to Wednesday 3 November 2010 inclusive of the Opening and Closing Ceremonies. Weather wise the city experiences an October mean temperature minimum 17.2 degrees centigrade and maximum 31.3 degrees centigrade with humidity ranging from 31 to 78% for the October and November months.

The Delhi Games Village is to be constructed as a low rise medium development on a 40 acre site in the heart of the capital with a possible capacity for 8,500 athletes and officials. Existing and new stadia will be used to house the following sports: Aquatics, Athletics, Badminton, Bowls, Boxing, Cycling, EAD Events, Gymnastics, Hockey, Netball, Rugby 7s, Shooting, Squash, Table Tennis and Weightlifting.

Delhi won the right to host the 2010 Games by defeating the Canadian city of Hamilton by 46 votes to 22 at the CGF General Assembly held in Montego Bay in November.2003.

To get the latest on preparations for the Games follow the link on the left to the official Games website for Delhi 2010 as well as clicking on the links below to read the Delhi and Hamilton Bid documents and CGF Bid Evaluation Report.

7

Olympic Games

The first Olympic Style games for athletes with a disability were held in Rome in 1960 which became the Paralympic Games. The first Winter Paralympics were held in Örnsköldsvik, Sweden in 1976. The Games are now always held alongside the Olympic Games as of June 19, 2001 when an agreement was signed between the International Olympic Committee (IOC) and the International Paralympic Committee (IPC) securing this practice for the future. The IPC logo denotes three Tae-Geuks, one in red, blue and green. The three Tae-Geuks symbolise the most significant components of the human being: Mind, Body, Spirit. "Mind, Body, Spirit" was adopted as the IPC motto.

The next Paralympic Games are going to be held in Athens, Greece from 17th to 28th September 2004. These will be the 12th Paralympic Summer Games. Four thousand athletes will participate, representing 145 countries in nineteen sports. A record number of broadcasters will be present to cover the Athens 2004 Paralympics, though the events will not be broadcast in the United States. Previous Paralympics have also suffered from limited broadcast and sponsorship.

The name derives from the Greek "para" ("beside" or "alongside"), and has nothing do do with paralysis or paraplegia.

Summer Games

1960 Summer Paralympic Games

The 1960 Summer Paralympic Games were the first Paralympics. They were held in Rome, Italy with the Olympics. The only disability included in this paralympics was spinal cord injury.

Games of the I Paralympics

Nations participating	23
Athletes participating	400
Events	57 in 8 sports
Opening ceremonies	September 18, 1960
Closing ceremonies	September 25, 1960
Officially opened by	Camillo Giardina

Medals Tally

Rank	Country	Gold	Silver	Bronze	Total
1	United States	29	7	7	43
2	Great Britain	19	16	18	53
3	France	15	1	3	19
4	Australia	11	4	1	16
5	Rhodesia	10	1	2	13
6	Belgium	8	1	0	9
7	Ireland	4	0	0	4
8	German Federal Republic	3	6	9	18
9	Italy	2	29	25	56
10	Austria	2	9	10	21
11	Netherlands	2	6	0	8
12	Malta	2	4	3	9
13	Switzerland	2	4	0	6
14	Norway	1	4	4	9
15	Israel	1	2	2	5
16	Finland	1	0	0	1
17	Argentina	0	3	2	5

1964 Summer Paralympics

The 1964 Summer Paralympics were the 2nd Paralympic Games to be held. They were held in Tokyo, Japan.

Games of the II Paralympics

Nations participating	21
Athletes participating	375
Events	144 in 9 sports
Opening ceremonies	November 3, 1964
Closing ceremonies	November 12, 1964

Medals Tally

Rank	Country	Gold	Silver	Bronze	Total
1	United States	50	41	31	122
2	Great Britain	18	23	19	60
3	Italy	14	15	24	53
4	Australia	11	11	8	30
5	Rhodesia	10	5	2	17
6	South Africa	8	8	3	19
7	Israel	7	3	10	20
8	Argentina	6	15	16	37
9	Germany	5	2	3	10
10	Netherlands	4	6	3	13
11	France	4	2	4	10
12	Austria	4	1	4	9
13	Japan	1	5	3	9
14	Belgium	1	0	2	3
15	Switzerland	0	1	0	1
16	Malta	0	0	2	2
17	Sweden	0	0	1	1

1968 Summer Paralympics

The 1968 Summer Paralympics were the third Paralympic Games to be held. They were originally planned to be held alongside the Summer Olympics in Mexico City, but in 1966, the Mexican government decided against it, due to difficulties. The Israeli government then offered to host the games in Tel Aviv.

Games of the III Paralympics

Nations participating	29
Athletes participating	750
Events	181 in 10 sports
Opening ceremonies	November 4, 1968
Closing ceremonies	November 13, 1968
Officially opened by	Yigal Allon

Medals Tally

Rank	Country	Gold	Silver	Bronze	Total
1	United States	33	27	39	99
2	Great Britain	27	21	20	68
3	Israel	17	21	25	63
4	Australia	15	16	7	38
5	France	14	9	9	32
6	Italy	13	10	15	38
7	German Federal Republic	12	12	11	35
8	Netherlands	12	4	4	20
9	Argentina	11	10	10	31
10	South Africa	9	10	7	26
11	Canada	6	6	7	19
12	Rhodesia	5	8	7	20
13	Norway	5	3	1	9
14	Jamaica	3	1	1	5
15	Austria	2	6	11	19
16	Japan	2	2	8	12
17	Sweden	1	6	4	11

(Contd...)

18	Ireland	1	5	5	11
19	New Zealand	1	2	1	4
20	Spain	0	4	0	4
21	Belgium	0	3	3	6
22	Switzerland	0	2	6	8

1972 Summer Paralympics

The 1972 Summer Paralympics were the fourth Paralympic Games to be held. They were held in Heidelberg, Germany.

Games of the IV Paralympics

Nations participating	41
Athletes participating	1,004
Events	187 in 10 sports
Opening ceremonies	August 2, 1972
Officially opened by	Dr. Gustav Heinemann

Medals Tally

Rank	Country	Gold	Silver	Bronze	Total
1	Germany	28	15	24	67
2	United States	17	28	28	73
3	South Africa	16	12	13	41
4	Great Britain	15	15	20	50
5	Netherlands	14	13	11	38
6	Poland	14	12	7	33
7	France	10	8	12	30
8	Israel	9	10	9	28
9	Italy	8	3	5	16
10	Jamaica	8	3	4	15
11	Australia	6	9	10	25
12	Canada	6	6	8	20
13	Austria	6	6	5	17

(Contd...)

14	Sweden	5	5	5	15
15	Japan	4	5	3	12
16	Rhodesia	3	5	4	12
17	New Zealand	3	3	3	9
18	Switzerland	3	2	3	8
19	Korea	3	2	1	6
20	Argentina	2	5	3	10
21	Ireland	2	4	2	8
22	Norway	1	5	5	11
23	Belgium	1	2	2	5
24	Yugoslavia	1	1	2	4
25	India	1	0	0	1
26	Kenya	1	0	0	1
27	Spain	0	4	1	5
28	Finland	0	2	2	4
29	Hong Kong	0	1	1	2
30	Hungary	0	0	1	1
31	Russia	0	0	1	1

1976 Summer Paralympics

The 1976 Summer Paralympics were the fifth Paralympic Games to be held. They were held in Toronto, in the province of Ontario, Canada.

The Paralympics in Canada and Toronto

1976 was the first time Canada has hosted the Paralympics, subsequently Canada will host the 2010 Winter Paralympics in Vancouver. Coincidentally, Montreal hosted the 1976 Summer Olympics. Toronto has in later years failed to win the Summer Olympics and Paralympics. Losing the bid for the 2008 Summer Olympics (2008 Summer Paralympics) was seen as being a boost to the Vancouver 2010 Winter Olympics bid.

Games of the V Paralympics

Athletes participating	1,657 (1,404 men, 253 women)
Events	447 in 13 sports
Opening ceremonies	August 3, 1976
Closing ceremonies	August 11, 1976

Medals Tally

Rank	Country	Gold	Silver	Bronze	Total
1	United States	66	44	45	155
2	Netherlands	45	25	14	84
3	Israel	39	13	16	68
4	Germany	37	33	26	96
5	Great Britain	29	29	36	94
6	Canada	25	26	26	77
7	Poland	24	17	12	53
8	France	23	22	14	59
9	Sweden	22	27	25	74
10	Austria	18	16	17	51
11	Australia	16	18	8	42
12	Mexico	16	14	9	39
13	Finland	12	20	18	50
14	Japan	10	6	3	19
15	Switzerland	9	12	10	31
16	Norway	9	6	4	19
17	South Africa	7	9	12	28
18	Belgium	7	7	8	22
19	New Zealand	7	1	5	13
20	Egypt	5	2	1	8
21	Ireland	4	10	6	20
22	Spain	4	6	2	12

(Contd...)

23	Argentina	3	4	6	13
24	Denmark	3	0	3	6
25	Italy	2	5	11	18
26	Indonesia	2	1	4	7
27	Korea	1	2	1	4
28	Burma	1	1	1	3
29	Peru	1	0	2	3
30	Hong Kong	0	1	2	3
31	Brazil	0	1	0	1
32	Guatemala	0	0	1	1

1980 Summer Paralympics

The 1980 Summer Paralympics were the sixth Paralympic Games to be held. They were held in Arnhem, Netherlands.

Games of the VI Paralympics

Nations participating	42
Athletes participating	1,973
Events	489 in 12 sports
Opening ceremonies	June 21, 1980
Officially opened by	Princess Margriet

Medals Tally

Rank	Country	Gold	Silver	Bronze	Total
1	United States	62	58	54	174
2	Germany	61	47	41	149
3	Canada	53	27	31	111
4	Poland	51	51	47	149
5	Great Britain	43	29	20	92
6	Netherlands	32	27	33	92

(Contd...)

7	Sweden	25	35	24	84
8	France	25	23	24	72
9	Mexico	20	16	4	40
10	Israel	12	18	11	41
11	Norway	11	11	7	29
12	Belgium	11	9	13	33
13	Austria	9	12	4	25
14	Switzerland	9	10	9	28
15	Australia	8	19	18	45
16	Japan	8	10	6	24
17	Finland	6	15	12	33
18	Italy	6	4	9	19
19	New Zealand	5	6	5	16
20	Jamaica	5	6	4	15
21	Egypt	4	7	3	14
22	Argentina	4	4	6	14
23	Yugoslavia	3	5	9	17
24	Denmark	3	4	6	13
25	Ireland	2	2	10	14
26	Kuwait	2	2	1	5
27	Iceland	2	0	1	3
28	Spain	1	14	9	24
29	Korea	1	2	1	4
30	Kenya	1	2	0	3
31	India	1	1	0	2
32	Indonesia	1	0	4	5
33	Colombia	1	0	1	2
34	Sudan	1	0	0	1
35	Zimbabwe	0	7	4	11
36	Bahamas	0	1	2	3
37	Hong Kong	0	0	2	2
38	Czechoslovakia	0	0	1	1
39	Greece	0	0	1	1
40	Malta	0	0	1	1

1984 Summer Paralympics

The 1984 Summer Paralympics were the seventh

Paralympic Games to be held. They were held in Stoke Mandeville, United Kingdom (wheelchair athletes) and New York, United States of America (cerebral palsy, visually impaired, amputee and les autres).

Games of the VII Paralympics

New York celebration

Nations participating	45
Athletes participating	1,800
Events	~300 in 15 sports
Opening ceremonies	June 17, 1984
Closing ceremonies	June 30, 1984
Officially opened by	Ronald Reagan

Stoke Mandeville celebration

Nations participating	41
Athletes participating	1,100
Events	~300 in 10 sports
Opening ceremonies	July 22, 1984
Closing ceremonies	August 1, 1984
Officially opened by	HRH Prince Charles

Medals Tally

Rank	Country	Gold	Silver	Bronze	Total
1	United States	101	91	84	276
2	Great Britain	75	80	85	240
3	Sweden	51	30	22	103
4	Canada	48	52	49	149
5	Germany	44	42	29	115
6	Netherlands	44	40	17	101
7	France	37	39	23	99
8	Australia	29	38	26	93

(Contd...)

9	Norway	22	24	20	66
10	Denmark	22	6	11	39
11	Spain	21	8	12	41
12	Poland	20	15	13	48
13	Finland	15	10	17	42
14	Ireland	13	11	20	44
15	Hungary	12	12	3	27
16	Belgium	9	11	6	26
17	Yugoslavia	7	9	8	24
18	Austria	5	13	7	25
19	Switzerland	5	2	2	9
20	Portugal	4	2	7	13
21	Italy	3	7	6	16
22	Japan	3	2	5	10
23	China	2	12	8	22
24	Israel	2	6	7	15
25	New Zealand	2	3	1	6
26	Egypt	2	0	3	5
27	Trinidad and Tobago	2	0	1	3
28	Luxembourg	1	4	1	6
29	Brazil	1	3	2	6
30	Burkina Faso	1	1	2	4
31	Mexico	0	3	3	6
32	Iceland	0	2	6	8
33	German Democratic Republic	0	2	1	3
34	India	0	2	1	3
35	Indonesia	0	1	1	2
36	Zimbabwe	0	1	0	1
37	Hong Kong	0	0	1	1
38	Korea	0	0	1	1

1988 Summer Paralympics

The 1988 Summer Paralympics were the first Paralympics, for 24 years, that were held along side the Olympics. They took place in Seoul, South Korea.

Games of the VIII Paralympics

Nations participating	61
Athletes participating	3,053
Events	729 in 16 sports
Opening ceremonies	October 15, 1988
Closing ceremonies	October 24, 1988
Officially opened by	Roh Tae-Woo

Medals Tally

Rank	Country	Gold	Silver	Bronze	Total
1	United States	92	91	85	268
2	Germany	77	64	48	189
3	Great Britain	62	66	51	179
4	Canada	54	42	57	153
5	France	45	48	49	142
6	Sweden	42	38	22	102
7	Korea	40	35	19	94
8	Netherlands	30	23	29	82
9	Denmark	25	18	22	65
10	Australia	23	34	37	94
11	Poland	22	25	34	81
12	Russia	21	19	15	55
13	Spain	18	13	12	43
14	China	17	17	9	43
15	Italy	16	15	27	58
16	Japan	16	12	17	45

(Contd...)

17	Belgium	15	17	9	41
18	Israel	15	13	15	43
19	Ireland	13	13	18	44
20	Austria	13	7	15	35
21	Switzerland	12	12	10	34
22	Finland	11	23	15	49
23	Norway	11	11	13	35
24	Mexico	8	9	6	23
25	Brazil	4	9	14	27
26	Kuwait	4	6	8	18
27	Yugoslavia	4	4	11	19
28	Iran	4	1	3	8
29	Portugal	3	4	5	12
30	New Zealand	2	4	11	17
31	Iceland	2	2	8	12
32	Bulgaria	2	1	0	3
33	Jamaica	1	4	3	8
34	Faroe Islands	1	3	3	7
35	Egypt	1	2	3	6
36	Puerto Rico	1	2	0	3
37	Bahrain	1	1	1	3
38	Guatemala	1	0	0	1
39	Argentina	0	7	2	9
40	Hungary	0	4	7	11
41	Kenya	0	4	1	5
42	Hong Kong	0	2	7	9
43	Greece	0	1	3	4
44	Indonesia	0	1	0	1
45	Czec and Esl Federal Republic	0	1	0	1
46	Thailand	0	1	0	1
47	Tunisia	0	0	2	2
48	Malta	0	0	1	1

1992 Summer Paralympics

The 1992 Summer Paralympics were the ninth Paralympic Games to be held. They were held in Barcelona, Spain.

Games of the IX Paralympics

Nations participating	82
Athletes participating	3,020
Events	487 in 15 sports
Opening ceremonies	September 3, 1992
Closing ceremonies	September 14, 1992

Medals Tally

Rank	Country	Gold	Silver	Bronze	Total
1	United States	76	51	48	175
2	Germany	60	50	60	170
3	Great Britain	40	46	41	127
4	France	36	35	33	104
5	Spain	34	31	42	107
6	Canada	28	21	26	75
7	Australia	24	27	25	76
8	Unified Team	17	14	15	46
9	Netherlands	13	15	11	39
10	Norway	13	12	7	32
11	Denmark	12	22	12	46
12	China	11	7	7	25
13	Korea	10	14	18	42
14	Italy	10	7	18	35
15	Finland	8	6	11	25
16	Poland	7	10	7	24
17	Japan	7	8	15	30
18	Switzerland	6	16	12	34
19	Sweden	5	22	8	35
20	Austria	5	4	13	22

(Contd...)

21	Belgium	5	4	6	15
22	Egypt	5	4	4	13
23	New Zealand	5	1	0	6
24	Czec and Esl Fed.R.	4	3	6	13
25	Hungary	4	3	4	11
26	Ind.Paralympians4	3	1	8	
27	South Africa	4	1	3	8
28	Hong Kong	3	4	4	11
29	Cuba	3	3	3	9
30	Portugal	3	3	1	7
31	Iceland	3	2	12	17
32	Brazil	3	0	4	7
33	Israel	2	4	5	11
34	Slovenia	2	0	1	3
35	Nigeria	2	0	0	2
36	Kuwait	1	3	1	5
37	Iran	1	2	1	4
38	Bulgaria	1	2	0	3
39	Panama	1	2	0	3
40	Argentina	1	1	0	2
41	Kenya	1	0	1	2
42	Lithuania	0	4	3	7
43	Ireland	0	3	3	6
44	Estonia	0	2	1	3
45	Greece	0	2	1	3
46	Mexico	0	1	10	11
47	Jamaica	0	1	2	3
47	Malaysia	0	1	2	3
49	Faroe Islands	0	1	0	1
50	Bahrain	0	0	1	1
51	Chinese Taipei	0	0	1	1
52	Croatia	0	0	1	1
53	Iraq	0	0	1	1
54	Thailand	0	0	1	1
55	Venezuela	0	0	1	1

1996 Summer Paralympics

The 1996 Paralympic Games in Atlanta, USA were the first Paralympics to get mass media sponsorship.

Games of the X Paralympics

Nations participating	103
Athletes participating	3,195(2,415 men, 780 women)
Events	508 in 20 sports
Opening ceremonies	October 15, 1996
Closing ceremonies	October 26, 1996
Officially opened by	Al Gore

Medals Tally

Rank	Country	Gold	Silver	Bronze	Total
1	United States	46	46	65	157
2	Australia	42	37	27	106
3	Germany	40	58	51	14
4	Great Britain	39	42	41	122
5	Spain	39	31	36	106
6	France	35	29	31	95
7	Canada	24	21	24	69
8	Netherlands	17	11	17	45
9	China	16	13	10	39
10	Japan	14	10	12	36
11	Poland	13	2	8	35
12	South Korea	13	2	15	30
13	Sweden	12	14	10	36
14	Italy	11	20	15	46
15	South Africa	10	8	10	28
16	Russia	9	7	11	27
17	Norway	9	7	4	20
18	Switzerland	9	6	6	21
19	New Zealand	9	6	3	18
20	Iran	9	5	3	17
21	Egypt	8	11	11	30
22	Belgium	8	10	7	25

(Contd...)

23	Cuba	8	3	0	11
24	Denmark	7	17	17	41
25	Austria	6	6	10	22
26	Portugal	6	4	4	14
27	Hong Kong	5	5	5	15
28	Iceland	5	4	5	14
29	Hungary	5	2	3	10
30	Finland	4	5	4	13
31	Mexico	3	5	4	12
32	Estonia	3	4	2	9
33	Belarus	3	3	7	13
34	Lithuania	3	2	6	11
35	Nigeria	3	2	3	8
36	Czech Republic	2	7	1	10
37	Brazil	2	6	13	21
38	Argentina	2	5	2	9
39	Slovakia	2	4	5	11
40	Algeria	2	2	3	7
41	Yugoslavia	2	2	0	4
42	Côte d'Ivoire	2	0	0	2
42	Panama	2	0	0	2
44	Ukraine	1	4	2	7
45	Ireland	1	3	6	10
46	Greece	1	1	3	5
47	Kuwait	1	1	1	3
48	Kenya	1	1	0	2
49	Chinese Taipei	1	0	2	3
50	Dominican Rep.	1	0	0	1
50	Peru	1	0	0	1
52	Israel	0	4	5	9
53	Slovenia	0	2	3	5
54	Tunisia	0	2	0	2
55	Bulgaria	0	1	1	2
56	Jordan	0	1	0	1
57	Moldova	0	0	2	2
57	Thailand	0	0	2	2
59	Jamaica	0	0	1	1
59	Uruguay	0	0	1	1

2000 Summer Paralympics

Games of the XI Paralympics

Nations participating	127
Athletes participating	3,843(2,867 men, 979 women)
Events	551 in 20 sports
Opening ceremonies	October 18, 2000
Closing ceremonies	October 29, 2000
Officially opened by	William Deane
Lit the Torch	Louise Sauvage

Medals Tally

Rank	Country	Gold	Silver	Bronze	Total
1	Australia	63	39	47	149
2	Great Britain	41	43	47	131
3	Spain	39	30	38	107
4	Canada	38	33	25	96
5	United States	36	39	34	109
6	China	34	22	17	73
7	France	30	28	28	86
8	Poland	19	22	12	53
9	South Korea	18	7	7	32
10	Germany	15	42	38	95
11	Czech Republic	15	15	13	43
12	Japan	13	17	11	41
13	South Africa	13	12	13	38
14	Russia	12	11	12	35
15	Netherlands	12	9	9	30
16	Iran	12	4	7	23
17	Mexico	10	12	12	34
18	Italy	9	8	10	27

(Contd...)

19	Denmark	8	8	14	30
20	Switzerland	8	4	8	20
21	Hong Kong	8	3	7	18
22	Nigeria	7	1	5	13
23	Egypt	6	11	11	28
24	Brazil	6	10	6	22
25	New Zealand	6	8	4	18
26	Portugal	6	5	4	15
27	Tunisia	6	4	1	11
28	Belarus	5	8	10	23
29	Sweden	5	6	10	21
30	Thailand	5	4	2	11
31	Ireland	5	3	1	9
32	Hungary	4	5	14	23
33	Greece	4	4	3	11
34	Cuba	4	2	2	8
35	Ukraine	3	20	14	37
36	Slovakia	3	5	5	13
37	Israel	3	2	1	6
38	Algeria	3	0	0	3
39	Austria	2	7	6	15
40	Norway	2	6	7	15
41	Iceland	2	0	2	4
42	Belgium	1	4	4	9
43	Finland	1	3	6	10
44	Chinese Taipei	1	2	4	7
45	Estonia	1	1	3	5
46	Kenya	1	1	2	4
47	Azerbaijan	1	1	0	2
47	Peru	1	1	0	2
47	Azerbaijan	1	1	0	2

(Contd...)

49	Côte d'Ivoire	1	0	1	2
50	Bulgaria	1	0	0	1
50	Jordan	1	0	0	1
50	Zimbabwe	1	0	0	1
53	Faroe Islands	0	3	1	4
53	United Arab Emirates	0	3	1	4
55	Argentina	0	2	3	5
56	Slovenia	0	2	2	4
57	Lithuania	0	2	1	3
58	Kuwait	0	1	4	5
59	Bahrain	0	1	1	2
59	Panama	0	1	1	2
61	Bosnia and Herzegovina	0	1	0	1
61	Yugoslavia	0	1	0	1
63	Latvia	0	0	3	3
64	Libya	0	0	1	1
64	Palestine	0	0	1	1
64	Philippines	0	0	1	1
64	Puerto Rico	0	0	1	1
64	Venezuela	0	0	1	1

2004 Summer Paralympics

The 2004 Summer Paralympic Games, the twelfth Paralympics, were held in Athens, Greece from September 17 to 28. The Paralympic Summer Games are the second-largest sporting event in the world, after the Summer Olympic games. An estimated 4,000 athletes took part, with ages ranging from 11 to 66.

The 800 m Women's Wheelchair Race and 1500 m Men's Wheelchair Race were the first competitions held for the 2004 Summer Paralympics, and also occurred during the 2004 Summer Olympics as demonstration sports. These races are now open to able-bodied people. See Wheelchair racing at the 2004 Summer Olympics for more details.

Athletes with learning difficulties are excluded from the games due to the difficulties in testing for and classifying these disabilities. The exclusion was introduced after the 2000 Summer Paralympics in Sydney, the first games with events exclusively for people with learning difficulties, after it was found that the majority of the Spanish basketball team were not disabled. The IPC has said that the exclusion will continue until there are sufficient tests for the disabilities and a way to measure the effect they have on a sport. Exhibition matches for these categories will still continue in basketball and table tennis. There is a separate games designed particularly for athletes with learning difficulties called the Special Olympics.

Medals Tally

Rank	Country	Gold	Silver	Bronze	Total
1	China	63	46	32	141
2	Great Britain	35	30	29	94
3	Canada	28	19	25	72
4	United States	27	22	39	88
5	Australia	26	38	36	100
6	Ukraine	24	12	19	55
7	Spain	20	27	24	71
8	Germany	19	28	32	79
9	France	18	26	30	74
10	Japan	17	15	20	52

Opening Ceremony

The opening ceremony for the 2004 Summer Paralympics took place on September 17, 2004. The show started with children passing on knowledge and raising their lights to the sky. This was a reference to Hippocrates, who transferred knowledge to the children. A 26 meters tall olive tree symbolising life stood in the middle of the arena. The opening ceremony also featured a performance with human drama, with light and with music, in an allegory about obstacles and limits.

The Parade of Delegations was accompanied by music of French composers Yves Stepping and Jean Christophe. The music told the legend of Hephaestos, god of fire and son of Zeus and Hera. An athlete from Turkmenistan propelled himself around the stadium by doing somersaults. Greece, the home team, received a strong cheer. After that, fireworks erupted at the stadium. There were 150 local support staff involved and 400 volunteers. The children were from ages 8 to 17, coming from Australia, France, Spain, Greece and Germany.

The Games were officially declared opened by Greek president Costis Stephanopoulos and Phil Craven, the president of the International Paralympic Committee. They were accompanied by the head of the organizing committee Gianna Angelopoulos-Daskalaki. Gianna Angelopolous told the athletes and the audience: "The Olympic flame illuminates athletes. Many of you will leave Athens with medals, but all of you will leave as champions." Phil Craven quoted Democritus in his speech: "Two thousand years ago, Democritus said 'To win oneself is the first and best of all victories.' This holds true for all athletes, but especially for Paralympians. Recognising and cultivating your unique abilities and mastering challenges - you set standards and give expression for many people, young and old, around the world." The Olympic flame was lit by Greek athlete Georgios Toptsis.

Closing Ceremony

The closing ceremony for the 2004 Summer Paralympics took place on September 28, 2004. The traditional cultural dislay was removed from the ceremony as a mark of respect for the deaths of 37 teenagers and 4 teachers from Farkadona, travelling to Athens, whose bus collided with a lorry near the town of Kamena Vourla. "The Athens Olympics Organising Committee [ATHOC] has decided to cancel the closing ceremony of the 12th Paralympics as initially planned and scheduled because of the tragic accident that cost the life of pupils," it was announced in a statement. "The artistic and entertainment part of the ceremony will not take place." Flags were flown at half mast and a minute's silence was observed.

In contrast with the formal nature of the operning ceremony, the athletes entered the stadium for the final time as a collective. The flag of the International Paralymic Committee was then officially handed over to the 2008 hosts, Beijing. A procession of young people then made their way to join the athletes in the centre of the stadium carrying paper lanterns, before the Paralympic flame was extinguished, the final moment of the Paralympic Games.

Sports played in 2004 Paralympic Games ,with results

The 2004 Paralympic Games included 19 sports. New categories for these games were five-a-side blind football, sitting volleyball for women, and Quads wheelchair tennis. The sports played were:

- Archery
- Athletics (including Wheelchair Racing)

- Boccia (see Boccia for details of this sport)
- Cycling
- Equestrian
- Football (5-a-side)
- Football (7-a-side)
- Goalball (see Goalball for details of this sport)
- Judo
- Powerlifting
- Sailing
- Shooting
- Swimming
- Table Tennis
- Volleyball (Sitting)
- Wheelchair Basketball
- Wheelchair Fencing
- Wheelchair Rugby
- Wheelchair Tennis

Nations

Athletes from 136 nations competed in the Athens Paralympics.

2008 Summer Paralympics

The 2008 Summer Paralympic Games will be the thirteenth Paralympics and they will be held in Beijing, China.

Winter Paralympics

1976 Winter Paralympics

The 1976 Winter Paralympic Games were the first winter Paralympics. They were held in Örnsköldsvik, Sweden.

The disabilities included in this paralympics were blindness and amputees. Fourteen countries took part with 250+ athletes.

Medals Tally

Rank	Country	Gold	Silver	Bronze	Total
1	West Germany	9	12	6	27
2	Switzerland	9	1	1	11
3	Finland	8	7	7	22
4	Sweden	6	7	7	20
5	Austria	5	16	14	35
6	Norway	5	3	2	10
7	Czechoslovakia	3	0	0	3
8	France	2	0	3	5
9	Canada	1	0	2	3

1980 Winter Paralympics

The 1980 Winter Paralympic Games were the second winter Paralympics and they were held in Geilo, Norway.

1984 Winter Paralympics

The 1984 Winter Paralympic Games were the third winter Paralympics and they were held in Innsbruck, Austria.

1988 Winter Paralympics

The 1988 Winter Paralympic Games were the fourth winter Paralympics and they were held in Innsbruck, Austria. These were the last Winter Paralympics to be held separately from the Winter Olympics, the next cycle, in 1992, the Olympics and Paralympics were held together.

1992 Winter Paralympics

The 1992 Winter Paralympics were the first winter Paralympics to be held along side the Olympics.

1994 Winter Paralympics

Games of the XVII Winter Olympiad

Nations participating	31
Athletes participating	512
Events	5 sports
Opening ceremonies	March 10, 1994
Closing ceremonies	March 19, 1994
Officially opened by	His Majesty King Harald V
Lit the Flame	Cato Zahl Pedersen

Medals Tally

Rank	Country	Gold	Silver	Bronze	Total
1	Norway	29	22	13	64
2	Germany	25	21	18	64
3	United States	24	12	7	43
4	France	14	6	11	31
5	Russia	10	12	8	30
6	Austria	7	16	12	35
7	Finland	7	6	11	24
8	Sweden	3	3	2	8
9	Australia	3	2	4	9
10	New Zealand	3	0	3	6
11	Switzerland	2	9	5	16
12	Poland	2	3	5	10
13	Spain	1	6	3	10
14	Canada	1	2	5	8

(Contd...)

15	Netherlands	1	0	3	4
16	Denmark	1	0	2	3
17	Italy	0	7	6	13
18	Japan	0	3	3	6
19	Slovakia	0	3	2	5
20	Great Britain	0	0	5	5
21	Belgium	0	0	1	1
21	Czech Republic	0	0	1	1
21	Estonia	0	0	1	1
21	Liechtenstein	0	0	1	1

1998 Winter Paralympics

The Seventh Winter Paralympics were held alongside the Winter Olympics in Nagano, Japan.

Games of the VII Winter Paralympics

Nations participating	32
Athletes participating	571
Opening ceremonies	March 5, 1998
Closing ceremonies	March ??, 1998
Officially opened by	Crown Prince Naruhito
Athlete's Oath	Yonoe Ryuei
Lit the Flame	Maruyama Naoya

Medals Tally

Rank	Country	Gold	Silver	Bronze	Total
1	Norway	18	9	13	40
2	Germany	14	17	13	44
3	United States	13	8	13	34
4	Japan	12	16	13	41
5	Russia	12	10	9	31

(Contd...)

6	Switzerland	10	5	8	23
7	Spain	8	0	0	8
8	Austria	7	16	11	34
9	Finland	7	5	7	19
10	France	5	9	8	22
11	New Zealand	4	1	1	6
12	Italy	3	4	3	10
13	Czech Republic	3	3	1	7
14	Ukraine	3	2	4	9
15	Canada	1	9	5	15
16	Australia	1	0	1	2
16	Denmark	1	0	1	2
18	Slovakia	0	6	4	10
19	Sweden	0	1	5	6
20	Netherlands	0	1	1	2
21	Poland	0	0	2	2

2002 Winter Paralympics

The 2002 Olympic Winter Games, including the 2002 Winter Paralympics, were held in Salt Lake City, Utah, United States.

Opening ceremonies held:	March 7, 2002
Closing ceremonies held:	March 16, 2002
Number of nations participating:	36
Number of athletes participating:	416
Persons who lit the Torch:	Muffy Davis and Chris Waddel

Medals Tally

Rank	Country	Gold	Silver	Bronze	Total
1	Germany	17	1	15	33
2	United States	10	22	11	43
3	Norway	10	3	6	19

(Contd...)

4	Austria	9	10	10	29
5	Russia	7	9	5	21
6	Canada	6	4	5	15
7	Switzerland	6	4	2	12
8	Australia	6	1	0	7
9	Finland	4	1	3	8
10	New Zealand	4	0	2	6
11	Italy	3	3	3	9
12	Spain	3	3	2	10
13	France	2	11	6	19
14	Czech Republic	2	1	2	5
15	Netherlands	1	3	0	4
16	Belarus	1	1	0	2
17	Poland	1	0	2	3
18	Ukraine	0	6	6	12
19	Sweden	0	6	3	9
20	Slovakia	0	3	6	9
21	South Korea	0	1	0	1
22	Japan	0	0	3	3

Sport for Development and Peace

The fundamental elements of sport make it a viable and practical tool to support the achievement of the Millennium Development Goals (MDGs). Sport has an impact on health and reduces the likelihood of many diseases. Sports programmes serve as an effective tool for social mobilisation, supporting health activities such as HIV/AIDS education and immunisation campaigns.

Sport can be a significant economic force, providing employment and contributing to local development. It is also a key site and natural draw for volunteer involvement. Furthermore, participation in sport supports the preservation of a clean and healthy environment. The practice of sport is vital to the holistic development of young people, fostering their physical and emotional health and building valuable social connections. It offers opportunities for play and selfexpression, beneficial especially for those young people with few other opportunities in their lives.

Sport also provides healthy alternatives to harmful actions, such as drug abuse and involvement in crime. Within schools, physical education is an essential component of quality education. Not only do physical education programmes promote physical activity; there is evidence that such programmes correlate to improved academic performance. Sport can cut across barriers that divide societies, making it a powerful tool to support conflict prevention and peace-building efforts, both symbolically on the global level and very practically within communities. When applied effectively, sports programmes promote social integration and foster tolerance, helping to reduce tension and generate dialogue. The convening power of sport makes it additionally compelling as a tool for advocacy and communications.

The world of sport presents a natural partnership for the United Nations system. By its very nature sport is about participation. It is about inclusion and citizenship. Sport brings individuals and communities together, highlighting commonalties and bridging cultural or ethnic divides. Sport provides a forum to learn skills such as discipline, confidence and leadership and it teaches core principles such as tolerance, cooperation and respect. Sport teaches the value of effort and how to manage victory, as well as defeat. When these positive aspects of sport are emphasised, sport becomes a powerful vehicle through which the United Nations can work towards achieving its goals.

The chief finding of the United Nations Inter-Agency Task Force on Sport for Development and Peace is that well-designed sport-based initiatives are practical and cost-effective tools to achieve objectives in development and peace. Sport is a powerful vehicle that should be increasingly considered by the United Nations as complementary to existing activities. The Task Force therefore strongly recommends that:

– Sport should be better integrated into the development agenda.
– Sport should be incorporated as a useful tool in programmes for development and peace.
– Sport-based initiatives should be included in the country programmes of United Nations agencies, where appropriate and according to locally assessed needs.
– Programmes promoting sport for development and peace need greater attention and resources by Governments and the United Nations system.
– Communications-based activities using sport should focus on well-targeted advocacy and social mobilisation, particularly at the national and local levels.
– A final recommendation of the Task Force is that the most effective way to implement programmes that use sport for development and peace is through partnerships.

MDGs and Sports Education

Education is central to the achievement of all of the MDGs, and sport has a natural place in education, whether the approach used is formal, non-formal or informal. In schools, physical education is a key component of a quality education and can be used to promote schooling among young people. Outside the classroom, sport is a "school for life", teaching basic values and life skills important for holistic development. Sport is also a powerful vehicle for public education, while sporting events can effectively increase awareness and galvanise support and action around key issues.

Sport is an ideal school for life: The skills learned through play, physical education and sport are fundamental to the holistic development of young people. These skills, such as cooperation and confidence, are essential for social cohesion and are carried throughout adult life. Sport actively educates young people about the importance of certain key values, such as honesty, fair play, respect for self and others, and adherence to the rules and respect for their importance. It provides a forum for them to learn how to cope with competition, not only how to lose but also how to win.

Sport is a way to build understanding for the value of common bonds. And traditional games, those native to an area or culture, can be especially effective in this regard. For example, some benefits of encouraging traditional games are that they emphasise the importance of diversity, contribute to inclusion and help people understand their own identity and those of others. Traditional sports and games are also usually lower in cost in terms of facilities and equipment than common sports.

Since 2000, Youth Education through Sport (YES), a sport and education programme led by youth for youth, has reached 25,000 young people in Zimbabwe's 10 provinces. Each participant must make a commitment to stay in school and to volunteer in the community. The aim of the programme is for young people to adopt life skills, become peer educators and contribute to their communities as positive role models. It is imperative that sports programmes both in and out of school include all people and ensure equal opportunity to participate regardless of gender, ethnicity or ability.

Girls, education and sport: The skills and values learned through sport are especially important for girls, given that they have fewer opportunities than boys for social interaction outside the home and beyond family networks. Ensuring that girls receive equitable access to quality education is central to development. Since achieving education for all and reaching girls who are denied access to basic education means expanding the way education is provided, non-formal forms of provision such as sportrelated programmes should be considered.

In Romania, UNICEF's education programme is using sport to increase school participation among the Roma community. The project aims to motivate children to attend school regularly as well as improve the gender balance in education by providing an opportunity for girls and boys to participate in sports teams, conditional upon school attendance and academic performance. Through sport, girls are given the chance to be leaders and improve their confidence and selfesteem. As girls begin to participate in sport, they also acquire new interpersonal links and access to new opportunities, allowing them to become more engaged in school and community life.

Sport provides young people with their own space, both physically and emotionally, which is especially important for girls. Sports teams and leagues often provide girls a forum to develop a sense of camaraderie and share time and values with other girls. Providing girls with access to sport can also contribute to achieving gender parity in education. Given that sport is a traditionally male domain, girls' participation in sport challenges stereotypes of girls and women, breaking down entrenched attitudes. And, as female athletes gain recognition, they become mentors for others.

Physical education and the disabled: Giving young people with disabilities the opportunity to participate in physical education programmes at school and through community clubs is crucial given the additional benefits they receive from sport and physical activity.

Sport, education and refugees: Education is voluntary for most refugees given that they are not citizens in their host countries. Sports programmes in refugee schools provide an additional incentive to get young people to school. Including physical education and team sports programmes in refugee schools attracts new groups of students to school, often girls, that otherwise do not attend. Sports programmes increase attendance rates and reduce antisocial and uncooperative behaviour, including violence.

Since 1997, IOC and UNHCR have been working in Bhutanese refugee camps in Nepal to offer struct u red sport and re c reational activities for refugees. By providing the opportunity to play, the programme aims to improve the education in the camps, while also helping to heal the psychological effects of war and flight.

UNHCR is working closely with many partners to provide refugees with sports activities in refugee communities around the world. In Peshawar, UNHCR partners with the NGO Right To Play and Insan Foundation Pakistan to provide sports and physical education programmes to Afghan refugees. The prog rammes contribute to the rise in school attendance rates, especially among girls, and, according to parents and teachers, reduce aggression and violence.

Physical education is an essential component of quality education and an integral part of lifelong learning. The neglect of physical education reduces the quality of education, with negative future impacts on public health and health budgets. Physical education is the only subject in the curriculum that focuses specifically on the body. In doing so, it helps teach young people respect for the body-their own as well as others- and helps them respond to many of the challenges faced by young people, including the threat of HIV/AIDS and other sexually transmitted diseases, and the dangers of tobacco and drugs. Providing students with the opportunity to play sport at school ensures that they receiveawell - rounded education that addresses body, mind and spirit.

Physical education is an effective means of promoting physical activity among young people. Given that rates of physical activity tend to decrease from adolescence, it is imperative that young people gain an appreciation of sport at school in order to ensure lifelong active and healthy living. In Mongolia, a UNESCO project funded by the Danish aid agency promotes sport at several learning centres throughout the country and supports physical education and sports events as part of the education curriculum. Inside the classroom, there is strong evidence highlighting the positive correlations between participation in sport and academic achievement.

One study found that children between the ages of 6 and 12 who do at least five hours per week of physical activity achieve better marks than those who are active for less than one hour. More generally, research shows that increasing the time spent on physical education in schools does not reduce marks in intellectual subjects but rather improves the ability of some students to learn and retain information. Despite recognition of the positive impact sport has on education and child development, physical education is being increasingly marginalised in the education system. This includes a decrease in the amount of time allocated to physical education, the number of specially trained staff, the amount of training for physical education teachers and spending on resources needed to participate in sport, physical activity and games in school.

Research conducted in 126 countries shows that the marginalisation of physical education is near universal. The primary reason for this marginalisation is that physical education is often seen as non-productive and non-intellectual and, hence, an inessential component of education, despite being a legal requisite in over 100 of the countries surveyed. In January 2003, UNESCO hosted representatives from 103 countries at a Ministerial Round Table. One of the three key topics addressed was the importance of reversing the marginalisation of physical education, given its effectiveness as a tool for health and physical development as well as for acquiring values necessary for social cohesion and intercultural dialogue.

Physical education is an excellent means to put into practice many of the skills that are considered necessary outcomes of a modern education system, especially teamwork, cooperation, problem-solving and confidence-building. These are aspects of learning that involve knowledge, but knowledge alone is not sufficient; physical education provides a very practical way to imbue these skills.

Development and Peace Challenges

Sport is far more than a luxury or a form of entertainment. Access to and participation in sport is a human right and essential for individuals of all ages to lead healthy and fulfilling lives. Sport-from play and physical activity to organised competitive sport-has an important role in all societies. Sport is critical to a child's development. It teaches core values such as cooperation and respect. It improves health and reduces the likelihood of disease. It is a significant economic force providing employment and contributing to local development. And it brings individuals and communities together, bridging cultural or ethnic divides. Sport offers a cost-effective tool to meet many development and peace challenges, and help achieve the Millennium Development Goals (MDGs).

The potential of sport as a tool for development and peace has yet to be fully realised. The use of sport remains outside the mainstream of thinking among United Nations agencies. While sport and play are repeatedly acknowledged as a human right, they are not always seen as a priority and have even been called the "forgotten right". Sport is seen as a by-product of development, not as an engine.

The potential links between sport and peace are also powerful. From international events to the grass roots, sport brings people together in a way that can cross boundaries and break down barriers, making the playing field a simple and often apolitical site for initiating contact between antagonistic groups. Consequently, sport can be an ideal forum for resuming social dialogue and bridging divides, highlighting the similarities between people and breaking down prejudice. The popularity of sport and its convening power further contribute to sport being a powerful voice for communicating messages of peace and a site for symbolic public acts on the global and local levels.

Sport is an effective element in community-based initiatives that aim to create sustainable peace. The skills and values learned through sport are many of the same skills and values taught in peace education to resolve and prevent conflict and create conditions conducive to peace, from the interpersonal to the international. Well-crafted sports activities teach respect, honesty, communication, cooperation , empathy, and how and why to adhere to rules. Sport is a powerful way to communicate these values, especially to young people, in a way that is fun and participatory. For refugees, displaced persons, orphans and former child soldiers, sport offers a sense of normality providing structure in destabilising environments, and serves as a means to channel energies positively.

Sport is an international language. Its ability to cross cultures enables sport-related programmes to bridge social and ethnic divides. As a result, sport can be a powerful tool to promote peace, both symbolically on the global level and very practically within communities. The power of sport can be used as a tool for preventing conflict as well as an element for building sustainable peace. When applied effectively, sports programmes promote social integration and foster tolerance. These core values are the same as those necessary for lasting peace. In post-conflict environments in particular, this can work to reduce tensions and generate dialogue.

The use of sport to promote peace is extremely effective in programmes at the community level, since they directly involve those affected by conflict and social tension. Sport is often denied in times of instability and yet it offers a sense of normality, especially for young people. Sports programmes provide structure in an unstructured and destabilising environment and serve as a means to channel energies away from aggression or self-destruction. Concurrently, they help build the individual skills and values necessary to avoid conflict and to ensure peace. Various groups benefit particularly from sportfor-peace programmes.

In Somalia, UNICEF and UNESCO are working towards promoting peace through sport with programmes that both train youth in peaceful conflict resolution skills while doing sports training and provide resources and encourage and support inter-district and regional sport-peace tournaments. The aim is to build the capacity of sport while creating a protective environment to help rehabilitate and reintegrate young people living in a post-conflict situation. In many circumstances young people lack hope, as well as the practical means to change their situation. Sport is a medium to help build character and confidence, preparing young people to better meet the challenges of a competitive world. These elements can be especially beneficial in the care and support of orphans.

The psychosocial benefits from the practice of sport help to address the trauma of flight and the distress resulting from displacement. Sports programmes serve as a positive and productive activity for refugees and internally displaced persons, easing many of the problems they face, including violence, limited access to education and broken family structures. Sport is used as a bridge between refugee and host communities, providing an opportunity for the communities to engage in positive activities. For example, in Thailand, "friendly matches" we re coordinated by UNHCR between refugee communities from the Tham Him camp and the local people fro m Suan Phung.

Child soldiers are uprooted from their communities and social structures and experience extreme brutality. The process of their demobilisation and rehabilitation is difficult and highly sensitive, requiring physical, psychological and psychosocial care, as well as opportunities to develop the skills necessary for adult life. Here, sport can play a unique role. Sports programmes offer a space to play, giving children back their childhood, while providing an outlet for channelling anger and controlling aggression. Sports teams also allow these young people to build positive connections with peers and adults, creating a sense of belonging that is essential for their effective demobilisation.

In Sierra Leone, UNICEF partners with the NGO Right To Play to incorporate sport and play into its Community Based Reintegration programme. Volunteers are working with local communities to build a net work of coaches who will implement sports programmes and provide young people with a sense of belonging through the establishment of crucial community connections.

Sport and Sustainable Human Development

Central to the United Nations notion of development is sustainable human development, which recognises that development is more than economic growth. Development is a process of enlarging people's choices and increasing the opportunities available to all members of society. Based on the principles of inclusion, equity and sustainability, emphasis is on the importance of increasing opportunities for the current generation as well as generations to come.

The basic human capabilities that are necessary for this are to "lead long and healthy lives, to be knowledgeable, to have access to the resources needed for a decent standard of living and to be able to participate in the life of the community". Sport can directly help build these capabilities. Participation in sport has significant physical benefits, contributing to people's ability to lead long and healthy lives, improving well-being, extending life expectancy and reducing the likelihood of several major non-communicable diseases, particularly heart disease, diabetes and certain cancers.

Sport also provides psychosocial benefits, such as fostering social integration and teaching coping mechanisms, as well as psychological benefits, such as reducing depression and improving concentration. Sport further builds human capabilities by increasing knowledge and contributing to education. Incorporating physical education into the school curriculum and providing opportunities for recreation improve a child's ability to learn, with evidence indicating that it also increases attendance and overall achievement.

Sport also educates people about the body, raising awareness and respect for their bodies and those of others, critical for healthy living and the prevention of diseases, like HIV/AIDS. Similarly, participation in outdoor sports raises awareness and respect for the environment, teaching people about the importance of a clean and healthy environment. Sport is also a key component of social life, directly engaging communities. It brings people together in a fun and participatory way. It helps create social relationships, build connections and improve communication between individuals and groups. Sport also mobilises volunteers and promotes active community involvement, helping to build social capital and strengthen the social fabric.

Effective development must be sustainable and human-centred. Sustainable development requires that the needs of the present generation are met without compromising the ability of future generations to meet their own needs, and human development requires that people's choices are enlarged, providing all members of society with increased opportunities and the conditions necessary to live long and fulfilling lives. Well-designed sports programmes work to assist meeting the objectives of sustainable human development, by contributing to economic and social development and environmental sustainability.

Sport and Social Development

More than stimulating economic growth, effectively designed sports programmes strengthen basic human capabilities, create connections between individuals, and teach core values and life skills. They are a valuable tool to initiate social development and improve social cohesion, especially when implemented with young people. Together, the benefits from such programmes provide a powerful means to tackle social exclusion, rehabilitate child labourers and integrate marginalised groups into their communities.

In Zambia, Edusport Outreach International uses netball, basketball, athletics, aerobics, dance and volley - ball programmes to train young people in coaching their peers and to teach life skills to over 10,000 street children, orphans and at-risk youth. The success of this programme has led to its being used as a model for programmes in Botswana, South Africa, Tanzania and Uganda.

Drug abuse

When social and personal skills are combined, sport can be an effective medium to intervene in a person's decision to abuse or not abuse drugs. While participation in sport does not inherently lead to a drug-free lifestyle, well-designed sports programmes, run by skilled and credible coordinators, help to reduce high-risk behaviours. This is especially true when the elements of sport are combined with the structured provision of drug-related information and life-skills training.

In 2001, the US National Basketball Association and a number of other partners cooperated in a high-profile camp for young teens from the former Yugoslavia. The camp focused on leadership building, conflict resolution and the importance of living a healthy lifestyle without drugs. In Georgia, more than 46,000 children from 2,028 schools have participated in regional football tournaments sponsored by government agencies, UNICEF, businesses and NGOs. The matches are designed to encourage a healthy lifestyle for young people, promoting the message that "smoking, drinking and taking drugs can't compare to the extraordinary high of kicking a winning goal".

Crime

Factors that contribute to young people turning to crime include the absence of positive role models, a lack of self-discipline and boredom. Sport can tackle these causes of juvenile crime by helping disaffected youth make positive connections with adults and peers, by integrating them into constructive activities within society and by providing a useful activity for their time.

In the UK, a recent report showed that sports programmes in high-crime areas helped reduce juvenile crime, vandalism and delinquency and stopped many young people from reoffending. In Brazil, UNICEF supports a detention centre for young people in trouble with the law. After academic classes, they play football, learn judo and practise gymnastics, helping them to channel frustrations and learn new ways to deal with anger.

Gender Equity

Sport can be an effective tool for empowering girls and women, given that they are often excluded from participating and enjoying the physical and psychosocial benefits offered by sport. By directly challenging and dispelling misperceptions about women's capabilities, integrated sports programmes help to reduce discrimination and widen the role prescribed to women.

In the US, research shows that regular participation in sport correlates to girls being less sexually active, lower rates of teen pregnancy and higher academic performance.

In Zimbabwe, IDSP, a division of Commonwealth Games Canada, partners with provincial health units to deliver biweekly aerobics programmes, open to all women in urban and rural communities and reaching an estimated 200,000 participants. Included are discussions on women's rights, parental guidance, basic health, family planning, pre- and post-natal care, HIV/AIDS education and counselling services.

Sport can integrate persons with disabilities into society, providing an arena for positive social interaction, reducing isolation and breaking down prejudice. Sports programmes for the disabled are also a cost-effective method of rehabilitation. They are highly therapeutic, improving motor skills and increasing mobility, self-sufficiency and self-confidence. The Norwegian Confederation of Sport and Olympic Committee (NIF) supports sports programmes for the disabled. For example, in Zimbabwe it is working with the Zimbabwe Olympic Committee and Common wealth Sport Development Programme (now IDSP) to assist people with disabilities, enabling them to participate in a sport of their choice.

Child Labour

As part of a quality education, sport can help to rehabilitate child labourers, strengthening their capacities, serving as part of a replacement activity to work and giving them the opportunity to play. Sport can also be used as a platform to mobilise young people within the community against child labour.

Sport and the Environment

The relationship between sport and the environment includes both the impact of sport on the environment and the impact of the environment on sport. All sports activities, events and facilities have an impact on the environment, creating an "ecological footprint". Although sport is generally not a major cause of pollution, its cumulative impact is significant and can include pesticides, erosion, waste generation and habitat loss. As a result, the negative impact of sport on the environment should always be minimised.

UNEP is working with major sports organisations, including the Olympic Movement and the World Federation of the Sporting Goods Industry, to ensure that major sports events and sports goods are "green". It is also important for sport to be pursued in an environmentally sustainable manner, given that the deterioration of environmental conditions reduces the health, well-being and living standards of individuals and communities as well as their levels of physical activity. Factors such as waterborne, airborne and soil-borne pollutants and ultraviolet radiation impact negatively on people's ability and willingness to participate in sport.

Conversely, a cleaner environment encourages people to be more connected to the natural environment and to be more physically active. Participation in sport also requires the provision of appropriate, safe and clean places to play, whether specific facilities or parks and open spaces. Maximising participation in sport therefore requires the creation of a clean, suitable and sustainable environment. The football club Mathare Youth Sports Association (MYSA), located in the slum of Mathare in Nairobi, allocates points to its teams on the basis of wins, losses, draws and garbage collection, coupling the health benefits from a clean environment with those from participation in sport.

The inherent link between a clean environment and participation in sport is part of what makes sport a powerful tool for communicating environmental messages and encouraging action to clean up the environment.

Sport and Volunteerism

Volunteers are an important strategic resource for sports programmes that should be actively mobilised. Sport everywhere relies on volunteers, whether community-based matches or international events. For example, the Sydney 2000 Olympic Games deployed 47,000 volunteers. Once involved through sport, volunteers can then be mobilised to donate their time to other activities. Given that sport is a key site for volunteer involvement, sport should be used to promote volunteerism, especially among youth whose participation is a strong predictor of volunteering in later life.

Volunteerism provides benefits to the individual, such as self-fulfilment, skill acquisition, increased understanding and social integration. It also benefits society, through impacts including economic growth, social welfare, community participation, generation of trust and reciprocity, and the broadening of social interaction through new networks. Consequently, volunteerism creates social capital, helping to build and consolidate social cohesion and stability. Sport is a key way to encourage volunteerism within societies and achieve the resulting social benefits.

In the UK, the contribution made by volunteers to sport is estimated to be greater than government and lottery funding combined. Volunteers are a key resource in sport for development programmes, including United

Nations Volunteers (UNVs), White Helmets (Argentina), Volunteer Service Organisation VSOs (UK), Peace Corps (US) and volunteer coaches used by NGOs including Sport Coaches' Outreach (SCORE) and Right To Play. SCORE, an NGO based in South Africa, recruits international and local volunteers to implement sports p ro g rammes in schools and in underprivileged communities. Volunteers work on activities including p hysical education programmes, organised sports activities in and after school, sports festivals, sport for the disabled and the development of community sports clubs. Key considerations regarding sport and development

- In order to maximise the economic potential of sport, development strategies should take an integrated, coherent approach, with emphasis placed on the value of stimulating growth at the local level. Sports programmes aimed at supporting social development must be well designed, led by trained personnel, focused on the development of the individual, and inclusive of all groups regardless of age, race, gender or ability.
- Consideration must be given to the potential harm or adverse effects of sports activities on the environment. The positive environmental achievements of sports organisations and the organisers of sports events should be recognised, as this can inspire others to increase their efforts in support of a sustainable environment.
- Volunteers are a strategic resource that should be mobilised when implementing sport-for development programmes. Furthermore, sport is a key site and natural draw for volunteer involvement.

Sport as a Human Right

Sport is more than a practical method to achieve

development and peace. The opportunity to participate in and enjoy sport and play is a human right that must be promoted and supported. Sport and play are therefore not only a means, but also an end. Sport is a human right is explicitly embodied in article 1 of the Charter of Physical Education and Sport adopted by UNESCO in 1978. The charter states: "The practice of physical education and sport is a fundamental human right for all." It stresses that every person is entitled to participate in sport, including especially women, young people, the elderly and the disabled.

Similarly, a child's right to play is enshrined in article 31 of the Convention on the Rights of the Child, which recognises "the right of the child to rest and leisure, to engage in play and re c reational activities appropriate to the age of the child". This article also state that not only do children have the right to play; they also have the right to the provision of the opportunity to play, requiring States to "encourage the provision of appropriate and equal opportunities for cultural, artistic, recreational and leisure activity". Several other United Nations instruments also acknowledge the importance of access to and participation in sport, such as the Convention on the Elimination of All Forms of Discrimination against Women .

Similarly, ILO Conventions Nos. 138 and 182 concerning child labour require Governments to establish policies for the rehabilitation of child labourers. Here, sport is considered an effective policy tool. In spite of these international instruments, the right to sport and play is often denied. In many cases this is because of discrimination, particularly by gender and ability. It is also frequently due to political neglect of the importance of sport in society, exemplified by the decline in spending on physical education and the lack of appropriate spaces and resources necessary for sport.

However, the fact that access to and participation in sport and play are human rights creates the responsibility to ensure that these rights are upheld. It places a duty on Governments, the United Nations system and others to ensure that the opportunity for participation in sport and play exists, allowing all people to enjoy their right to sport and play.

Sport is one of the world's most powerful communication tools due to its near universal appeal, its convening power and its many positive associations. Together, these features give sport the capacity to reach a range of audiences in a variety of ways, particularly groups that are otherwise difficult to reach. On its own, sport has the ability to communicate messages such as cooperation, coexistence, or how to graciously manage victory and defeat. As a powerful channel to communicate messages, sport can also be an arena to promote United Nations goals for development and peace. Whether a one-time event or a longer-term campaign, sport provides valuable opportunities for both advocacy and the mobilisation of communities.

Many United Nations organisations successfully collaborate with the world of sport in the area of communications, generating awareness about key issues through global and local efforts. There are various ways to apply sport as a vehicle to send messages, including working with athletes as ambassadors or spoke spersons, the dedication of sports events to development issues, the involvement of the media, and collaboration between all partners involved in sports events, including the private sector. These elements can be used individually, or together as part of a coherent communications framework.

The US-based Johns Hopkins University Center for Communication Programs partners with sports associations and health organisations in over 30 African countries to promote healthy lifestyles and behaviours. Health information booths are set up inside stadiums, educational materials are distributed, counselling services are offered, pre-match and half-time forums are held to advocate action, and male and female athletes serve as spokes persons at events and in the media.

Athletes as Goodwill Ambassadors: The popularity of sports stars allows them to effectively reach diverse audiences, as well as attract the media's attention. In addition to raising awareness about issues, athletes serving as spokespersons can generate the interest of fellow athletes and team members, and contribute to resource mobilisation efforts. At the global level, UNDP works with footballers Ronaldo and Zinédine Zidane, who act as Goodwill Ambassadors to advocate and support efforts for poverty reduction. At the local level, UNESCO and UNICEF collaborate in Cambodia to communicate HIV/AIDS prevention messages through a national poster campaign that highlights four well-known athletes in four different sports, including swimming, Khmer boxing, football and running.

Sports events: Sports events are an ideal forum for reaching large numbers of people, whether at the event or through its media coverage. Methods for raising awareness include using public service announcements, in-stadium videos and banners, half-time shows, publications and linkages on event web sites. Globally, sports events can incorporate all of the above elements and provide additional opportunities in marketing and fund-raising.

At the global level, UNICEF and FIFA formed an alliance to promote the "Say Yes for Children" campaign during the 2002 FIFA World Cup in Korea/Japan. Multiple elements we re used including public service announcements with footballers, information on child rights in publications and on FIFA's web site and the generation of funds through an auction of sports memorabilia. The alliance also resulted in collaboration between UNICEF country offices and national football federations in over 70 countries. At the community level, the NGO Comvida in Honduras uses national football matches as a communications tool to increase awareness about HIV/AIDS prevention, putting on mock games prior to matches featuring players like "Knowledge" and "Condom" as well as "Infected Syringe" and "Infidelity", representing "Death United".

Within sports organisations: Establishing strong relationships with sports federations and associations is an effective way to tap into existing networks and structures on regional and national levels, allowing a large and diverse audience to be reached with key United Nations messages. As sports organisations work to develop their sport at local levels, United Nations bodies can promote and support those areas where the development of sport overlaps with the use of sport-for-development issues. Furthermore, working directly with sports organisations can lead to positive changes and get them on board, setting high-profile examples for others to follow.

United Nations Environment Programme (UNEP's) work with International Olympic Committee (IOC) led to the environment becoming the third dimension of the Olympics-alongside sport and culture-and to the development of guidelines for "green" Olympic Games, with supplementary effects to other sports federations and associations and NOCs.

Sports media: The print and broadcast media are further avenues for advocacy through sport. Profiles of individuals who have been affected by sport, accounts that highlight charitable involvement of athletes, or stories that bring light to United Nations sport-related activities raise awareness about development issues.

Campaigns: Many United Nations communications campaigns use sport in a variety of innovative ways:

- ILO partners with FIFA and the African Confederation of Football (CAF) to promote the "Red Card to Child Labour" campaign, which at the 2002 African Cup of Nations in Mali used sponsors, the media and promotions at matches and national and local football events to spread its message.
- WHO dedicated 2002 World Health Day to "Move for Health" and 2002 World Tobacco Day to "Tobacco Free Sports" in collaboration with FIVB, FIFA (Tobacco - Free World Cup in Korea/Japan) and IOC (Tobacco - Free Salt Lake City 2002 Winter Olympic Games).
- UNDP's campaign "Teams to End Poverty" draws upon the advocacy power of sports stars including Ronaldo, Zinédine Zidane, Martina Hingis, Sergey Bubka and Jacques Villeneuve. UNEP's "Play for the Planet" campaign aims to bring young people closer to nature through sport and raise awa reness that sport and sports facilities can adve rsely affect the environment .
- UNHCR's "Wannabe" campaign in Argentina, Australia, Germany, Greece and Spain uses images of refugee children playing football to create empathy for refugees.
- UNICEF's alliances with FIFA (2003 Women's World Cup) and Fox Kids (Under-13 Fox Kids Cup) promote "25 by 2005", a campaign for girls' education aiming to get all girls in school and achieve gender parity in education in 25 countries by 2005.

- UNODC's "Sports against Drugs" public awareness campaign uses sports stars and sports events in over 40 countries to promote positive life choices and a drug-free lifestyle.

Sport is a particularly effective element to support social mobilisation efforts. The convening power of sport makes it a useful tool to gather communities for direct public initiatives. It allows for broad delivery of messages and programmes to a wide range of people at the local and national levels, drawing diverse groups of people together in a fun and supportive environment. Whether as an additional element to an existing sports event or as a sports festival specifically organised to support mobilisation efforts, sport platforms provide a practical and cost-effective medium to get critical information and programmes to hard-to-reach groups in a comfortable and familiar atmosphere.

In Nairobi, Kenya, the German Population Fund and UN-Habitat ran a football league for homeless young people at risk from prostitution, violence and HIV/AIDS. By gathering together over 1,000 streetchildren, the tournaments offered an entry point for organisations to provide services and support, highlighting the value of providing an enabling environment for sports activities that can then be used as a vehicle for outreach and social mobilisation.

As a valuable supplement to health initiatives, particularly immunisation campaigns, sport platforms are an effective way to bring adults and young people together in a friendly environment. They can attract people into district centres from surrounding regions, and increase the numbers of those reached with critical vaccines. In Ghana, a sports festival was organised by government ministries, WHO, UNICEF, the Vaccine Fund and Right To Play to mobilise rural communities in order to be immunised with the 5-in-1 vaccine. Key considerations regarding sport and communication

- Public campaigns should have clear strategies and focused objectives, and consideration should begiven to the various ways to use sport as a vehicle to send messages.
- When designing communications initiatives using sport, programme objective s, target audiences and the media to communicate must be clearly defined.
- Athletes who serve as spokes persons or ambassadors must reflect the values of the United Nations.
- Care should be taken when partnering with elite sport for communications purposes given potential conflicts of interest in getting the public and media's attention during "noisy events" and the potential commercialism involved.
- At the local and national levels, sport should also be considered as a highly effective tool to support social mobilisation efforts and a practical method of engaging diverse communities in broader activities, particularly in support of large-scale immunisation campaigns or other health initiatives.

Sports and Partnerships

The eighth MDG calls for the establishment of a global partnership for development as a way both to involve new sections of society and to meet global development challenges more effectively. The sports sector provides a significant opportunity for establishing such new partnerships for development. Partnerships are also a particularly effective way to work with sport, given that the world of sport is by definition a world of partnerships, incorporating diverse actors from the community, the public and private sectors and sports organisations at various scales.

The implementation of sport for-development programmes and the use of sport by the United Nations should, there fore, be based upon strategic partnerships with the range of stake holders involved in sport, coordinated through a common framework.

There are three areas where a partnership approach to sport for development is especially effective.

Programme implementation: Many existing sport-for-development programmes are based on innovative partnerships among actors in the sector, including sports organisations, government authorities, volunteers, and NGOs with specific expertise in implementing sport-related development programmes.

- UNDP has partnered with NOCs in over 50 countries since 1997 through various initiatives to fight poverty.
- WHO works with multiple levels of government in various countries to develop multisectoral policies necessary for effective "Move for Health" initiatives.
- In numerous countries, including Mozambique and Nicaragua, Universitas, a United Nations programme established by ILO, the Italian Government and a range of UN agencies, is tapping into the international network of universities to assist with the training and management aspects of sport and to actively address issues of knowledge-sharing and youth training in conjunction with efforts to enhance local development through sport.

Resource mobilisation: Partnerships provide a strategic approach to resource mobilisation, both for and through sport. They are an effective way to fund development initiatives for specific issues, and are useful instruments for government initiatives. Ways to mobilise resources include engaging sports organisations and athletes or forging partnerships and with the private sector. Corporate philanthropy efforts are particularly effective if working with sponsors of major sports events or focusing on causerelated marketing or other creative initiatives. The

Olympafrica Foundation funds centres throughout Africa that use sport to foster social development. Olympafrica operates in partnership with major donors including a number of UN agencies and international corporations, as well as community groups and partners at the local level. In Cuba, there are 41,000 tertiary-educated technical support and training personnel who are sports specialists. These people are a valuable resource in Cuba's technical cooperation programmes in over 100 countries, who can be working alongside medical personnel to address health and social issues through sport.

Advocacy: Partnering with the sports world also provides innovative ways to communicate the messages of the United Nations to diverse groups and to effectively mobilise society around certain issues.

A strategic approach should be developed in the United Nations system to foster field-based partnerships related to sport in a way that is both impact-oriented and cost-effective, as well as complementary to technical cooperation projects and broader development goals.

Sport and Health

Sport directly contributes to the pursuit of the Millennium Development Goals. It is an innovative and effective tool to assist existing efforts to achieve specific targets such as those concerning education, gender equality, HIV/AIDS and the reduction of major diseases.

More broadly, well-designed sports programmes are also a cost-effective way to contribute significantly to health, education, development and peace and a powerful medium through which to mobilise societies as well as communicate key messages. As one of the richest and most developed aspects of civil society, and as a powerful international network of private sector actors and organisations, sport opens new avenues for creative partnerships through which to achieve the Untied Nations development goals.

Sport and physical activity are essential for improving health and well-being, an aim integral to the achievement of the MDGs. Appropriate forms of sport and physical activity can play a significant role to prevent as well as help cure many of the world's leading non-communicable diseases. Evidence shows that regular participation in physical activity programmes provides all people with a wide range of physical, social and mental health benefits. Such active participation also complements strategies to improve diet, discourage the use of tobacco, alcohol and drugs and enhance functional capacity.

Consequently, physical activity is an effective method of disease prevention for the individual and, for nations, a cost-effective way to improve public health. The health burden from preventable non-communicable diseases, such as cardiovascular diseases, cancer, diabetes and chronic respiratory diseases, is increasing significantly throughout the world. WHO estimates that mortality, morbidity and disability resulting from these leading diseases currently account for approximately 60 per cent of all deaths and 43 percent of the global disease burden. These rates are expected to rise to 73 per cent and 60 per cent respectively by 2020.

Unhealthy diets, tobacco use and physical inactivity are the dominant factors causing the chronic diseases listed above and are now leading public-health issues in most countries. Of the disease-causing factors, physical inactivity is estimated to directly cause 1.9 million deaths globally, while also indirectly contributing to diseases and deaths resulting from factors including high blood pressure, high cholesterol and obesity.

Globally, over 60 per cent of adults do not participate in a sufficient amount of sport and physical activity, largely due to changes in lifestyle such as inactivity at work, sedentary forms of re creation, like television and computers, and excessive use of "passive" modes of transport. Such a sedentary lifestyle also contributes to obesity. Those most likely to be physically inactive are women, older people, the disabled and people from lower socio-economic groups. In addition, while physical activity is critical for the holistic development of young people, one third of adolescents are insufficiently active, with girls offered fewer opportunities to be active than boys. This is especially problematic given that patterns of physical activity set when young usually form the basis for lifelong activity.

Engaging in sport has multiple health benefits. Physical activity can reduce the risk both of dying prematurely from non-communicable diseases and of developing illnesses ranging from cardiovascular diseases, cancer and diabetes to stress, anxiety and depression. It also helps prevent and reduce hypertension, control body weight, prevent and control osteoporosis and manage chronic pain. While it is critical that everyone regularly participates in sport and physical activity, regardless of age, ability, gender or background, physical activity provides additional benefits to certain groups, for example:

- Among young people, physical activity contributes to healthy bones, efficient heart and lung function and improved motor skills and cognitive function.
- Among women, physical activity helps prevent hip fractures and reduce the effects of osteoporosis.
- Among older people, physical activity enhances functional capacity, helping maintain quality of life and independence.

SPORT AND HIV/AIDS

The HIV/AIDS pandemic is one of the greatest threats to life, dignity and the enjoyment of human rights. UNAIDS estimates that 42 million people are living with HIV/AIDS; 90 per cent are from developing countries, 75 per cent in sub-Saharan Africa. Fourteen million children have lost one or both parents to the disease. The extent of devastation caused by this pandemic makes it more than a health issue. HIV/AIDS has fundamental implications for economic development, social cohesion and security, which resonate throughout society. Consequently, all aspects of civil society, including sport, must be mobilised in the global fight against HIV/AIDS.

Sport can be a vehicle to help mitigate the spread and impact of HIV/AIDS. The four pillars necessary for effective HIV/AIDS programming are knowledge, life skills, the provision of a safe and supportive environment and access to services. The nature of sport and the benefits derived when it is incorporated into development initiatives make it well suited to support these four pillars. The groups most at risk of contracting the disease-women and young people, especially girls-are known to be highly responsive to targeted sports initiatives.

Knowledge: Coaches and leaders of sports programmes are well placed to incorporate HIV/AIDS prevention activities into sports programmes. Young people playing sport usually have a special and trusting relationship with their coaches, often unlike other relationships with adults. This puts coaches in a good position to discuss sensitive issues, especially sex, in a way necessary to effectively teach HIV/AIDS prevention and to care for those members who are HIV- positive.

Life skills: Well-designed sports programmes teach essential life skills necessary for HIV/AIDS protection and prevention, further enhancing the effectiveness of incorporating sport. Studies shows, for example, that when adolescent girls participate in sport, they develop a sense of ownership of and respect for their bodies, encouraging them to delay sexual activity.

Safe and supportive environment: Given the informal, social and fun nature of sport and play, the playing field can be readily transformed into a secure environment necessary for effective HIV/AIDS programmes and activities. Sport provides a forum to openly discuss the disease, its transmission and the eradication of stigma and discrimination. In particular, this is especially effective in the care and support of orphans and other vulnerable children, in that sport not only provides structure and connections with others but it also provides a space for expression and a chance to play.

Access to services: Sport is well placed to increase knowledge, provide life skills and create a safe environment. It is, therefore, an ideal location to access services, particularly for young people. Collaboration with sports organisations can tap into an existing network of clubs, volunteers and communication channels, providing a medium to engage large numbers of people quickly. "Kicking AIDS Out" is a regional network of organisations in southern Africa that uses sport to strengthen communities. It creates sustainable sports activities that increase awareness about HIV/AIDS, provide leadership training to at-risk youth and offer safe and healthy alternative activities.

The effectiveness of sport for communication and social mobilisation makes it a highly effective tool for raising public awareness about HIV/AIDS. Sports leagues and matches bring communities together, providing an ideal site for public information campaigns on prevention and protection and reaching large numbers of people of varying backgrounds and ages. Furthermore, sport's positive associations and the widespread perception that it is removed from formal politics means that these messages have the potential to reach populations who might not otherwise be reached. The participatory nature of sport also makes it a powerful means to dispel misunderstandings about the disease, breaking down stigma and discrimination.

Information about HIV/AIDS is not getting out and is especially not being absorbed by adolescents. Therefore, it is imperative to explore new and innovative ways to deliver prevention messages. The deep roots of sport within communities and its appeal to young people make it a positive forum for implementing HIV/AIDS prevention programmes. UNFPA supports the Botswana Christian Council and the Botswana National Sports Council as part of its efforts to promote reproductive health and HIV/AIDS prevention among adolescents. These two societal institutions we re chosen because of their significant influence on young people and high levels of youth participation, emphasising the power of sport to address the issue of HIV/AIDS.

The impact of HIV/AIDS on the world of sport will be dramatic, especially in high-incidence countries. HIV infection is concentrated among young people and the working-age population, the same groups that are most involved in sport. Sports organisations in high-incidence countries will increasingly be confronted by the fact that athletes, coaches, staff and members will become ill and die. Already HIV/AIDS absences, due to people becoming ill, attending funerals or caring for sick family members, are eroding many sports bodies and threatening them with organisational collapse.

While all organisations in high-incidence countries face this threat, sports organisations, like community-based groups and NGOs, are particularly vulnerable, given that they often rely on people with specialised skills and volunteers who can be difficult to replace. Sports organisations need to plan their response. This can include innovative thinking in the recruitment of new members, staff, coaches and volunteers. However, it should also include working with existing personnel to help prevent the spread of the disease and to mitigate its impact on those who are already infected or personally affected.

HIV-positive sportswomen and sportsmen must feel that they are in "safe havens" in their sports organisations. ILO, with UNAIDS, has developed a "Code of Practice on HIV/AIDS and the World of Work", as well as a "Tool Box for Young Workers on HIV/AIDS", a valuable resource for sports organisations.

8

International Charter of Physical Education and Sport

(Adopted by the General Conference at its twentieth session, Paris, 21 November 1978)

PREAMBLE

The General Conference of the United Nations Educational, Scientific and Cultural Organisation, meeting in Paris at its twentieth session, this twenty-first day of November 1978.

Recalling that in the United Nations Charter the peoples proclaimed their faith in fundamental human rights and in the dignity and worth of the human person and affirmed their determination to promote social progress and better standards of life,

Recalling that by the terms of the Universal Declaration of Human Rights everyone is entitled to all the rights and freedoms set forth therein without discrimination of any kind as to race, colour, sex, language, religion, political or other opinion, national or social origin, property, birth or other consideration,

Convinced that one of the essential conditions for the effective exercise of human rights is that everyone should be free to develop and preserve his or her physical, intellectual and moral powers, and that access to physical education and sport should consequently be assured and guaranteed for all human beings,

Convinced that to preserve and develop the physical. intellectual and moral powers of the human being improves the quality of life at the national and the international levels,

Believing that physical education and sport should make a more effective contribution to the inculcation of fundamental human values underlying the full development of peoples,

Stressing accordingly that physical education and sport should seek to promote closer communion between peoples and between individuals. together with disinterested emulation, solidarity and fraternity, mutual respect and understanding, and full respect for the integrity and dignity of human beings,

Considering that responsibilities and obligations are incumbent upon the industrialised countries and the developing countries alike for reducing the disparity which continues to exist between them in respect of free and universal access to physical education and sport,

Considering that to integrate physical education and sport in the natural environment is to enrich them and to inspire respect of the earth's resources and a concern to conserve them and use them for the greater good of humanity as a whole,

Taking into account the diversity of the forms of training and education existing in the world, but noting that, notwithstanding the differences between national sports structures, it is clearly evident that physical education and sport are not confined to physical well-being and health but also contribute to the full and well-balanced development of the human being,

Taking into account, furthermore, the enormous efforts that have to be made before the right to physical education and sport can become a reality for all human beings, Stressing the importance for peace and friendship among peoples of co-operation between the international governmental and non-governmental organisations responsible for physical education and sport, Proclaims this International Charter for the purpose of placing the development of physical education and sport at the service of human progress, promoting their development, and urging governments, competent non-governmental organisations, educators, families and individuals themselves to be guided thereby, to disseminate it and to put it into practice.

Article 1. The practice of physical education and sport is a fundamental right for all

1.1. Every human being has a fundamental right of access to physical education and sport, which are essential for the full development of his personality. The freedom to develop physical, intellectual and moral powers through physical education and sport must be guaranteed both within the educational system and in other aspects of social life.

1.2. Everyone must have full opportunities, in accordance with his national tradition of sport, for practising physical education and sport. developing his physical fitness and attaining a level of achievement in sport which corresponds to his gifts.

1.3. Special opportunities must be made available for young people, including children of pre-school age, for the aged and for the handicapped to develop their personalities to the full through physical education and sport programmes suited to their requirements.

Article 2. Physical education and sport for an essential element of lifelong education in the overall education system

2.1. Physical education and sport, as an essential dimension of education and culture, must develop the abilities, will-power and self-discipline of every human being as a fully integrated member of society. The continuity of physical activity and the practice of sports must be ensured throughout life by means of a global, lifelong and democratised education.

2.2. At the individual level, physical education and sport contribute to the maintenance and improvement of health, provide a wholesome leisure-time occupation and enable man to overcome the drawbacks of modern living. At the community level, they enrich social relations and develop fair play. which is essential not only to sport itself but also to life in society.

2.3. Every overall education system must assign the requisite place and importance to physical education and sport in order to establish a balance and strengthen links between physical activities and other components of education.

Article 3. Physical education and sport programmes must meet individual and social needs

3.1. Physical education and sport programmes must be designed to suit the requirements and personal characteristics of those practising them, as well as the institutional, cultural, socio-economic and climatic conditions of each country. They must give priority to the requirements of disadvantaged groups in society.

3.2. In the process of education in general, physical education and sport programmes must, by virtue of both their content and their timetables, help to create habits and behaviour patterns conducive to full development of the human person.

3.3. Even when it has spectacular features, competitive sport must always be in accordance with the Olympic ideal to serve the purpose of educational sport, of which it represents the crowning epitome. It must in no way be influenced by profit-seeking commercial interests.

Article 4. Teaching, coaching and administration of physical education and sport should be performed by qualified personnel

4.1. All personnel who assume professional responsibility for physical education and sport must have appropriate qualifications and training. They must be carefully selected in sufficient numbers and given preliminary as well as further training to ensure that they reach adequate levels of specialisation.

4.2. Voluntary personnel, given appropriate training and supervision, can make an invaluable contribution to the comprehensive development of sport and encourage the participation of the population in the practice and organisation of physical and sport activities.

4.3. Appropriate structures must be established for the training of personnel for physical education and sport. Personnel who have received such training must be given a status in keeping with the duties they perform.

Article 5. Adequate facilities and equipment are essential to physical education and sport

5.1. Adequate and sufficient facilities and equipment most be provided and installed to meet the needs of intensive and safe participation in both in-school and out-of-school programmes concerning physical education and sport.

5.2. It is incumbent on governments, public authorities, schools and appropriate private agencies, at all levels to join forces and plan together so as to provide and make optimum use of installations, facilities and equipment for physical education and sport.

5.3. It is essential that plans for rural and urban development include provision for longterm needs in the matter of installations, facilities and equipment for physical education and sport, taking into account the opportunities offered by the natural environment.

Article 6. Research and evaluation are indispensable components of the development of physical education and sport

6.1. Research and evaluation in physical education and sport should make for the progress of all forms of sport and help to bring about an improvement in the health and safety of participants as well as in training methods and organisation and management procedures. The education system will thereby benefit from innovations calculated to develop better teaching methods and standards of performance.

6.2. Scientific research, whose social implications in this sphere should not be overlooked, must be oriented in such a way that it does not allow of improper applications to Physical education and sport.

Article 7. Protection of the ethical and moral values of physical education and sport must be a constant concern for all

7.1. Top-class sport and sport practised by all must be

protected against any abuse. The serious dangers with which phenomena such as violence, doping and commercial excesses threaten its moral values, image and prestige pervert its very nature and change its educative and health promoting function. The public authorities, voluntary sports associations, specialised non-governmental organisations, the Olympic Movement, educators, parents, supporters' clubs, trainers, sports managers and the athletes themselves must combine their efforts in order to eliminate these evils. The media have a special role to play, in keeping with Article 8 in supporting and disseminating information about these efforts.

7.2. A prominent place must be assigned in curricula to educational activities based on the values of sport and the consequences of the interactions between sport, society and culture.

7.3. It is important that all sports authorities and sportsmen and women be conscious of the risks to athletes, and more especially to children, of precocious and inappropriate training and psychological pressures of every kind.

7.4. No effort must be spared to highlight the harmful affects of doping, which is both injurious to health and contrary to the sporting ethic, or to protect the physical and mental health of athletes, the virtues of fair play and competition, the integrity of the sporting community and the rights of people participating in it at any level whatsoever.

It is crucial that the fight against doping should win the support of national and international authorities at various levels, and of parents, educators, the medical profession, the media, trainers, sports managers, and the athletes themselves, to ensure that they abide by the principles set out in the existing texts, and more particularly the International Olympic Charter against Doping in Sport. To that end, a harmonised and concerted policy must guide them in the preparation and application of anti-doping measures and of the educational action to be undertaken.

Article 8. Information and documentation help to promote physical education and sport

8.1. The collection, provision and dissemination of information and documentation on physical education and sport constitute a major necessity. In particular, there is a need to circulate information on the results of research and evaluation studies concerning programmes, experiments and activities.

Article 9. The mass media should exert a positive influence on physical education and sport

9.1. Without prejudice to the right of freedom of information, it is essential that everyone involved in the mass media be fully conscious of his responsibilities having regard to the social importance, the humanistic purpose and the moral values embodied in physical education and sport.

9.2. Relations between those involved in the mass media and specialists in physical education and sport must be close and based on mutual confidence in order and sport and to ensure objective and well-founded information. Training of personnel for the media may include elements relating to physical education and sport.

Article 10. National institutions play a major role in physical education and sport

10.1. It is essential that public authorities at all levels and specialised non-governmental bodies encourage those physical education and sport activities whose educational value is most evident. Their action shall consist in enforcing legislation and regulations, providing material assistance and adopting all other measures of encouragement. stimulation and control. The public authorities will also ensure that such fiscal measures are adopted as may encourage these activities.

10.2. It is incumbent on all institutions responsible for physical education and sport to promote a consistent, overall and decentralised plan of action in the framework of lifelong education so as to allow for continuity and co-ordination between compulsory physical activities and those practised freely and spontaneously.

Article 11. International co-operation is a prerequisite for the universal and well-balanced promotion of physical education and sport

11.1. It is essential that States and those international and regional intergovernmental and non-governmental organisations in which interested countries are represented and which are responsible for physical education and sport give physical education and sport greater prominence in international bilateral and multilateral co-operation.

11.2. International co-operation must be prompted by wholly disinterested motives in order to promote and stimulate endogenous development in this field.

11.3. Through co-operation and the pursuit of mutual interests in the universal language of physical education and sport, all peoples will contribute to the preservation of lasting peace, mutual respect and friendship and will thus create a propitious climate for solving international problems. Close collaboration between all interested national and international governmental and non-governmental agencies, based on respect for the specific competence of each, will necessarily encourage the development of physical education and sport throughout the world.

Bibliography

Block, M. E., "What is appropriate physical education for students with profound disabilities?", *Adapted Physical Education Quarterly,* 1992.

_____________ ., "A Teacher's Guide to Including Students with Disabilities in General Physical Education", Baltimore, MD: Brookes Publishing Co., 2000.

_____________ ., Conatser, P., "Consulting in adapted physical education." *Adapted Physical Activity Quarterly,* 1999.

_____________ ., Rizzo, T. L., "Attitudes and attributes of physical education teachers towards including students with severe and profound disabilities into regular physical education", *Journal of The Association for Persons with Severe Handicaps,* 1995.

Bricker, D., "The challenge of inclusion." Journal of Early Intervention, 1995.

Broadhead, G. D., "Time passages in adapted physical education", In: G. A., Brooks (ed.), *Perspectives on the academic discipline of physical education,* Champaign, IL: Human Kinetics, 1981.

Craft, D. H., "Inclusion: Physical education for all." *Journal of Physical Education,* Recreation and Dance,. 1994.

Downing, J. E., "Including students with severe and multiple disabilities in typical classrooms", Baltimore: Paul H. Brookes, 1996.

_____________ ., Rebollo, J., " 'Parents' perceptions of the factors essential for integrated physical education programs." *Remedial and Special Education,* 1999.

Fiornini, J., Stanton, K., Reid, G., "Understanding parents and families of children with disabilities: Considerations for adapted physical activity." Palaestra, 1996.

Goldberg, B., (ed.), "Sports and exercise for children with chronic health conditions", Champaign, IL: Human Kinetics, 1996.

Heikinaro-Johansson, P., Sherrill, C. "Integrating children with special needs in physical education: A school district assessment model from Finland", *Adapted Physical Activity Quarterly,* 1994.

Henry, F.M., "The academic discipline of physical education." Quest, 1978.

Hodge S.R., Davis R., Woodard R., Sherill C., "Comparison of Practicum Types in Changing Preservice Teachers' Attitudes and Perceived Competence." *Adapted Physical Activity Quarterly,* 2002.

Hogan, P.I., "Problem based learning and personnel preparation in adapted physical education", *Adapted Physical Activity Quarterly,* 1990.

Lieberman, L.J., Houston-Wilson, C., "Strategies for inclusion: A handbook for physical educators", Champaign, IL: Human Kinetics, 2002.

Lienert, C., Sherrill, C., Myers, B., " 'Physical educators' concerns about integrating children with disabilities: A cross-cultural comparison", *Adapted Physical Activity Quarterly,* 2001.

Lytle R.K., Collier D., "The consultation process: adapted physical education specialists' perception." *Adapted Physical Activity Quarterly,* 2002.

Newell, K. M., "Physical activity, knowledge types, and degree programs", *Quest,* 1990.

Reid, G., Stanish, H. "Professional and disciplinary status of adapted physical activity". *Adapted Physical Activity Quarterly,* 2003.

Rink, J. E., "Teaching physical education for learning", St. Louis: Mosby, 1993.

Stanton, K., Colvin, A., "The physical educator's role in inclusion". 1996.

Index

Abdul Kalam , A.P.J., 163
Academic performance 239
Amarakosha 89
Ancient Olympics game 97
Archaeological excavations 101
Association Of National Olympic Committees of Africa (ANOCA) 161
Athens Olympics Organising Committee [ATHOC] 229

Ball games 79
Barbarian game 97
Board games 6

Card Games 6
Carl Lewis 118, 120
Centennial Olympic Park 122
Chandrababu Naidu 166
Chariot races 106
Chariot racing 106
Chaturanga 90
Christian civilization 97
Competitive sports 5
Confederation of Football (CAF) 258
Court of Arbitation for Sport (CAS) 127

Early Childhood Care and Education 253
Encyclopedia Britannica 90

Festival Games 81
Fictional setting 7

Gambling games 81
Game theory 79
Gladiatorial contests 100
Graceful human bodies 83
Guru-Shishya tradition 93
Gymnasia 84
Gymnasium 102
Gymnastics 8

Hellenic festival 98

Indian Olympic Association (IOA) 167
International Olympic Committee (IOC) 108, 207, 257
International Paralympic Committee (IPC) 207, 228

Javelin Throwing 105
Johns Hopkins 255
Judo 92

Kalaripayate 92
Kalaripayattu 158
Karate 92
Karnam Malleswari 158

Lal Bahadur Stadium 159
Ludwig Wittgenstein 3

Mahabharata 89
Mahatma Gandhi 158
Material possessions 88
Mathare Youth Sports Association (MYSA) 251
Mental acuity 8
Millennium Development Goals (MDGs) 243
Modern Olympic Games 107
Much-touted computerized scoring 122

National Olympic Committee 121

Oft-repeated argument 168
Olympiad 98
Olympic chariotrace 95
Olympic Games 104
Olympic history 116
Olympic tournament 125
Olympic victories 94
Olympic Village 111, 117
Online Games 7
Open-ended computer simulations 7
Opening ceremony 157

Palaestra 85
Panhellenic Games 101
Pankration 106
Paralympic Games 207
Pen-and-paper roleplaying games 7
Penathlon 106
Physical activity 1
Physical development 81
Political instability 155
Pragmatism 166
Pugilism 105

Record-setting 112
Recreational activity 1
Religious sacrifices 99
Role-playing Games 7

Semi-structured activity 1
Single-player computer game 4
Single-player Games 4
Sport Coaches' Outreach (SCORE) 253
Summer Paralympics 211
Sustainable human development 247

Temporary stitches 120
Traditional role playing games 8

United Nations Volunteers (UNVs) 252
Unusual fighting technique 103

Valery Borzov 113
Video Games 6
Vijayabhaskara Reddy 159

Warfare skills 8
Well-designed sports programmes 247
William Jones 89, 113
Winter Paralympics 232
Women's Wheelchair Race 226

Youth Education through Sport (YES) 238